*How To Books*

Writing
# Features & Interviews

How To Books are designed to help people achieve their goals. They are for everyone wishing to acquire new skills, develop self-reliance, or change their lives for the better. They are accessible, easy to read and easy to act on. Other titles in the series include:

**Writing for Publication**
*How to sell your work and succeed as a writer*

**Making Money from Writing**
*How to become a freelance writer*

**Writing Short Stories & Articles**
*How to write successfully for magazines and newspapers*

**Researching for Writers**
*How to gather material for articles, novels and non-fiction books*

**Writing Reviews**
*How to write about arts and leisure for pleasure and profit*

**Copyright & Law for Writers**
*How to protect yourself and your creative work*

The *How To Series* now contains around 250 titles in the following categories:

**Business & Management**
**Computer Basics**
**General Reference**
**Jobs & Careers**
**Living & Working Abroad**
**Personal Finance**
**Self-Development**
**Small Business**
**Student Handbooks**
**Successful Writing**

For full details, please send to our distributors for a free copy of the latest catalogue:

**How To Books**
Customer Services Dept.
Plymbridge Distributors Ltd, Estover Road
Plymouth PL6 7PZ, United Kingdom
Tel: 01752 202301   Fax: 01752 202331
www/howtobooks.co.uk

# Writing

# Features & Interviews

*How to build a career as a
freelance journalist*

**CHRISTINE HALL**
*2nd edition*

**How To Books**

Other books by the same author:

*How to Get a Job in Germany*
*How to Live and Work in Germany*
*Living & Working in Britain*
*Living & Working in China*
*How to Work in Retail (with Sylvia Lichfield).*

First published by How To Books Ltd, 3 Newtec Place,
Magdalen Road, Oxford OX4 1RE, United Kingdom
Tel: 01865 793806   Fax: 01865 248780
email: info@howtobooks.co.uk
www.howtobooks.co.uk

First edition 1995
Second edition 1999

British Library Cataloguing in Publication Data
A catalogue record for this book is available from
the British Library

Editing by Christine Kinsman
Cover design by Shireen Nathoo Design
Cover image PhotoDisc

Produced for How To Books by Deer Park Productions
Typeset by Concept Communications Ltd, Crayford, Kent
Printed and bound by Cromwell Press, Trowbridge, Wiltshire

NOTE: The material contained in this book is set out in good
faith for general guidance and no liability can be accepted
for loss or expense incurred as a result of relying in particular
circumstances on statements made in the book. The laws and
regulations are complex and liable to change, and readers should
check the current position with the relevant authorities before
making personal arrangements.

# Contents

# List of illustrations

# Preface
## to the Second Edition

Over 10,000 magazines and newspapers are published in the UK alone. This means a huge market for freelance writing, especially for features and articles.

Freelance journalism is a competitive field; but it is accessible to everyone. With hard work, determination, and the knowledge of what editors really want it is possible to earn good income from freelance writing. This book shows how to succeed.

Special thanks to everyone who helped with this book: writers Claire Gill, Diana Lloyd Taylor, Mary Victoria Webb, Lynda Rajan, Norman Toulson, Evelyn Thomsen, Mary Rensten, Molly Perham, Rosemary Wells, Jane Baker, Mike Gerrard and John Dawes for help with the first edition; Priscilla Burton, Colin Daniels, John Finch, Linda Cunniffe, Malcolm Cloke, Mary Sarkar for suggestions for the second edition; the students from my How to Write for Publication courses at Hastings College of Arts & Technology and at the Old Rectory Adult Education Residential College in Fittleworth for their 'reader profiles'; editors (feature editors, editorial assistants...) Rob Keenan of *Amateur Gardening*, Stephen Garnett of *Evergreen*, Mick Whitworth of *The Grocer*, Pam Gilder of *Countryside*, Amanda Griffin of *Stationery Trade News*, John T. Wilson of *Great Ideas*, Mary and Brian Lund of *Picture Postcard Monthly*, Charles Donavan of *Woman & Home*, and Frank Westworth of *Classic Bike Guide* for their comments and quotes.

The case studies are based on fictitious characters. They have been chosen to represent typical situations, but any similarity of names is coincidence. The magazines used for sample letters exist only in the imagination of the author. Of course, the editors who give their generous advice at the end of most chapters are real people as you will see when you study their magazines.

*Christine Hall*

# 1

## Planning Your Success

Freelance journalism is one of the few hobbies which doesn't cost a lot of money. It can even be self-financing or profitable.

You can expand it into a freelance career: as a journalist you are independent, you can work from home, meet interesting people and earn a good income.

Many would-be writers dream of this career, but few succeed. They are talented, and may even have a few **articles** published, but they cannot achieve the big break-through. Perhaps you are among them.

As an editor, I have accepted hundreds of articles for newspapers, trade and consumer magazines, and rejected thousands. I know that many of these aspiring writers could break into print and make regular sales if they had an idea of what editors really want.

### WHY WRITE ARTICLES?

There are almost 10,000 magazines and newspapers published in the UK alone, and most of them buy freelance manuscripts.

It is easier to break into print with articles than with short stories, and it is easier to make a living too. Most magazines publish only one story per issue, but dozens of articles, and most newspapers and trade magazines carry only articles. Editors can reprint a good short story after many years, but an article, however well written, becomes outdated, so the editor has to buy up-to-date material.

### WHY DO EDITORS USE FREELANCES?

In a difficult economic climate, when publishers face losses in both advertising and subscription revenue, editorial budgets are cut back to a minimum. Less money is available to a constantly increasing number of aspiring contributors, including redundant staff journalists. Established writers receive less **commissioned** work, and newcomers find it almost impossible to break into the market. A hopeless situation? Certainly not.

Clever freelances can secure a share of the reduced editorial budget if they are aware of what type of **features** editors are looking for in difficult times.

The first contributions to be axed are the beautifully written ones – those which editors used to accept because of their witty or elegant style. Most of them are based on facts and anecdotes obtained from reference books. Staff journalists can write them better and cheaper.

Your sales will be affected far less if you have expert knowledge of a topic. You don't need a university degree in your subject: your experience in bringing up a handicapped child, in organising camping holidays for teenagers, or in repairing furniture, makes you an expert.

For the editor, it is cheaper to buy a feature from a knowledgeable freelance than to assign a staff writer to spend days or weeks on research.

## Do you have what it takes?

Your success depends on four factors:

1.  Natural writing talent.

2.  Learning the craft and the necessary skills.

3.  Hard work, dedication and self-discipline.

4.  Business sense and marketing skills.

You need some of each, but not necessarily in equal parts. If you are born with extraordinary writing talents, you need less time to learn the skills. If you are only modestly talented, you need more dedication and must concentrate more on learning the craft. If you don't have the self-discipline to write a lot, you can make up for it by using your excellent marketing skills to sell every piece you write.

There is little you can do about your natural writing talent. The more you possess, the easier it is to succeed.

The craft of writing articles, journalistic skills, as well as the business and marketing side, are aspects you can learn from this book.

Hard work, dedication and self-discipline are what you have to put into it yourself. For many aspiring journalists, the difference between success and failure lies in six words: 'I did not have the time.'

## GETTING STARTED

All you need to set yourself up as a journalist is a typewriter, a pile of A4 paper, envelopes, stamps, a notebook and a pen, and access to a telephone.

Reference books, word processors, answering machines, headed paper and so on are useful, but not essential. You can add them as you earn money from your journalism. (See Chapter 12: Going Freelance.)

## LEARNING THE CRAFT

This book teaches you all you need to know about the craft to get started as a journalist. If you enjoy the additional stimulation of a course, there are several possibilities.

### Evening classes

Classes at a college or adult education centre don't cost a lot (about £35 for a term), and you get comments on your work from both the tutor and other participants. Set tasks motivate you to write regularly, and meeting other writers can be stimulating.

However, course tutors are rarely successful writers themselves. They can point beginners in the right direction, but advanced writers may get little out of the lessons. Courses tend to emphasise the pleasure of creativity more than professionalism, and you may spend time learning about areas of writing in which you are not interested.

### Residential courses

If you need to get away from your daily environment (for example, from looking after small children) to concentrate on writing, residential weekend or one-week courses are ideal. They allow you to immerse yourself in the subject without distraction. Many of these courses look at specific aspects of writing, for example, travel writing, or features.

However, they are relatively expensive (around £130 for two and a half days) because you pay for meals and accommodation as well as for the tuition.

A regular organiser of writing weekends is The Old Rectory, Fittleworth, Pulborough, West Sussex RH20 1HU, Tel/Fax: (01798) 865306. Other organisers advertise their courses in writing magazines and daily newspapers.

### Correspondence courses

You get your tuition by post and don't waste your writing time travelling to classes, and you can fit your studies into your daily routines. Correspondence courses are ideal for those who are bound to the house, for example handicapped people or parents of small children.

You have specified tasks to complete, and your tutor comments on your work and suggests improvements.

The course material is usually very good, but the success depends on your input. Learning by correspondence requires self-discipline and stamina; many students drop out.

Some organisers offer courses which cover the whole world of writing, including romantic novels and writing for children. You will

**John's tale:**

*'I signed up for a correspondence course with a college which promised to refund course fees if students didn't earn their money back from their writing. I did not earn money from writing articles while on the course and it was a long and protracted struggle to get a refund. Finally I succeeded, with the help of the newspaper where the advertisement for the course had been published.*

*I think I'd better not name the college, but I believe they've gone out of business anyway.*

*Undaunted, I continued to write and became a moderately successful part-time journalist, using my own initiative. I also wrote the book How to Be a Freelance Disc Jockey for How To Books Ltd.*

*I signed up for a correspondence course, this time with the Morris College of Journalism. It cost £270 (now the price has gone up to £290). This college claims that within having three articles published, you can recoup your enrolment fee of £270. But the most I ever got for an article was £50. So I sent them the proof of three recent articles for which I had received the sum of £95. They refunded the difference, straight away, without quibbling. I was amazed.*

*In addition, they asked me to write a testimonial which they could use for promotional purposes. I got paid £50 for that.*

*What's more, I found the course useful. I learned a lot and have some comprehensive notes all bound in smart folders. I'm sure they'll be a useful reference work in years to come. I only wish there had been more practical assignments.*

*John Clancy*

Fig. 1. A student's experience.

probably spending your time more effectively if you choose a shorter course which concentrates on journalism.

Expect a comprehensive journalism course to cost around £300. Here is a useful tip: Don't enrol immediately when you receive the information. Let a few weeks pass. Almost every correspondence course organiser will offer a substantially reduced rate to hesitating customers.

Try to talk to people who have already completed the course; their comments are invaluable. I have asked around and the course which received the best comments was the Morris College of Journalism – see Fig. 1. on page 14.

Their address is: Morris College of Journalism, The Old School, Princes Road, Weybridge, Surrey KT13 9DA, Tel: (01932) 850008, Fax: (01932) 850805.

## Criticism services

Some writers offer to read and criticise your work for a fee. This service is useful if you cannot get honest criticism from another source, for example if you suspect that your spouse and your neighbours praise your work because they are too kind to tell you the truth.

The advice is only as good as the person who gives it. Check out the consultant's experience both in providing criticism and in getting published.

Remember that criticism obtained from these sources will be honest, but not necessarily frank. No consultant wants to lose a client. Instead of saying 'This piece is poorly written and boring', they write:'This feature shows great potential for improvement. . .'.

Consultants show you how to structure your article better, how to make the most of quotes or how to trim the piece down to saleable length, but they cannot sell your work for you.

Professional advice is not cheap. Expect to pay around £20 per article (less if you send in several at the same time).

For your first attempts at writing, it is cheaper listening to the comments from the members of your writers' group. But once you've mastered the basics a professional's comments can be valuable.

Criticism services come and go. You find them in the classified advertisements of the writing magazines. Be careful before you part with your money. A surprising number of consultants are failed would-be writers, usually teachers of English, who do little more than point out the odd grammatical error. They can't sell their own work, so they try to earn money by telling other people how to do it. They may know less about selling articles than you do.

Ask what their own journalism qualifications are, request a list of their published work, and how long their consultancy has been trading.

## Writers' groups

Joining a writers' group is the cheapest way to get advice, honest and fair criticism, extra motivation and a boost to your social life. You can find out about writers' groups in the area from your local library or from the *Directory of Writers' Circles*. You can also start your own group.

Each writers' group works differently. Hastings Writers' Group, for example, meets every other week, either to discuss their own work, or for a talk given by a professional writer. Tunbridge Wells Writers' Circle organises monthly talks by VIP authors, and runs sub-groups for journalism, short stories, novels and poems. Darenth Writers in Sevenoaks meet monthly to read aloud their latest work and invite comments.

Many other writers' groups, however, are little more than coffee and gossip circles. If the members are not committed to writing, and if you haven't learnt anything at the end of a meeting, you are better off at home, writing.

## Postal workshops

If there is no writers' group in your area, you can join a postal group. Each time a parcel of manuscripts arrives, you take out your previous contribution, add your latest work, and write your opinion on the other people's work on a comment sheet. These postal workshops are great fun, and you get honest and fair criticism for little more than the cost of the postage stamps.

Depending on the size of the group and the efficiency of the members, it can take a while for the parcel to make a round.

## Writers' magazines

There are several excellent magazines for writers, and it is worth subscribing to at least one of them. Each time an issue arrives, crammed with ideas, advice, information on competitions and suggestions about where to sell your articles, your writing gets a big motivation boost.

On the whole, these magazines are most suitable for the enthusiastic beginner.

*Writers News* appears monthly and contains the most up-to-date information on writing competitions. *Writing Magazine* is aimed at beginners and is the only writing magazine you can buy at the newsagents. The *New Writer* is an amalgamation of the former magazines *Quartos* and *Acclaim*; it has a strong bias towards fiction writing and only touches on the subject of features. Several other good regional newsletters exist as well.

To save money, members of a writers' group can share a subscription, or persuade the local library to stock these magazines.

## OVERCOMING WRITER'S BLOCK

Writer's block is the name for the feeling that you cannot write anything, that you are empty, that you cannot come up with creative ideas or produce anything worth reading. Causes include tiredness, stress, great expectations or other pressures, lack of confidence or laziness.

Other languages have no phrase for this state of mind. Perhaps the writers in other countries don't suffer from this problem.

Strangely, the symptoms only affect freelance writers. Staff reporters never seem to have writer's block. They would not keep their jobs for long if they did.

Here are some tried and tested methods for overcoming writer's block.

- Set certain hours a day aside for writing every week. Lock the door, take the phone off the hook and sit down at your typewriter.

- Imagine that you are your own employer. Hire yourself for the day (or hour), and make sure that your employee gives his or her very best during this time.

- Imagine that you are a staff reporter and have to report to your editor or publisher at the end of the day.

- When you find it difficult to concentrate, go for a half-hour brisk walk, whatever the weather, to clear your mind. Then return to your typewriter.

- Whenever you go through a non-creative phase, use the time for all those essential non-writing activities: filing, writing query letters, sending invoices, research, market study.

- Set yourself a deadline. The average journalist is most productive writing under pressure.

## DEVELOPING YOUR PERSONAL FIVE-YEAR PLAN

Where do you want to be in five years? What do you want to have achieved by then? Close your eyes and imagine the situation. Write down every detail.

Then decide how much you want to achieve in each of the five years leading up to that big target. Write down your targets, leaving a lot of space to jot down ideas of how you can achieve them. Write down all ideas as they come over the next few months. This book will provide many suggestions.

**PHASE 1**
You learn the craft, picking up advice from professional journalists and from books.
Your target is to get as many pieces published as possible.
It does not matter what they are, where they appear or if you get paid for them.
Building your portfolio must be your priority.

When your portfolio contains at least ten published articles, move on to phase 2.

**PHASE 2**
Get as many articles published for payment as possible.
It does not matter how much you earn. If your payment is not more than £5 for an article in a small magazine, or a food hamper for the best readers' letter in a women's magazine, that's fine.

When you've had at least ten articles published for payment, move on to phase 3.

**PHASE 3**
Your aim is to get published in as many different magazines and newspapers as possible, with your byline.
Start specialising in one or several subjects. Join a writers' organisation and have headed paper printed.

Some editors recognise your name as a specialist writer and they value your contributions. Move on to phase 4.

**PHASE 4**
You develop gradually from a hobby writer to a professional. Concentrate on your best paying markets, and write mostly for them. Put a price on your work. Write only for publications which pay at least £20.

You know your markets and have built up contacts, and are selling your features regularly. You could say 'I'm a part-time writer'. Move on to phase 5.

**PHASE 5**
Learn marketing skills. Develop a business plan. Invest in basic office equipment. Increase your minimum rate to £50 per 1000 words. Try to break into markets which pay much more

You are a professional and ready to go freelance.

Fig. 2. Step by step from hobby writer to professional journalist.

The most successful strategy for a beginner to become a professional freelance journalist has five phases: see Fig. 2 on page 18.

## How long does it take?

It all depends on you, on how much time and effort you are willing to spend. Five years is a realistic target if you have a full-time job, or are looking after a family with small children, but dedicate most of your spare time to writing.

If you can apply yourself to writing full time, you can make it in two years. On the other hand, if you regard writing as a hobby you can spend more time on phases one, two and three, and skip phases four and five altogether.

## CASE STUDIES

### Matt

An 'A' level student who is determined to be a newspaper journalist, Matt knows that he won't find a junior reporter's job with a newspaper unless he has completed a course at journalism college, and that he won't get a place at college unless he has something to offer which other applicants don't have – such as a portfolio of published articles.

Matt is prepared to work hard and do a lot of writing in his spare time in order to have as many articles as possible published by next year, when he will apply for a college place. He will learn to touch type to produce professional-looking **manuscripts**.

### Cathy

This trained secretary and mother of three children wants to work from home. She needs the income, but also the flexible work hours which will allow her to look after her children, one of whom is disabled. She owns a word processor, and does some freelance secretarial work, but finds that mere typing doesn't satisfy her.

As far as she can remember, she has always been writing short stories, poems, letters and sketches. She has sent out some of her articles, but they all came back with rejection slips: 'The editor has read your article with interest, but regrets he cannot use it.'

Now Cathy wants to find out where she went wrong, and what editors really want. She considers signing up for a correspondence course. Her dream is to see her **byline** in a women's magazine.

### Nigel

A trained mechanic who has worked both in production and as a service engineer for household appliances, Nigel was made redundant two years ago. At 48 it seems that most employers consider him too old, and many refuse to take on a long-term unemployed person anyway.

One of his previous jobs had included writing user manuals for household appliances, and he knows that he is good at explaining technical matters in plain English. He has heard that technical authors earn well.

Nigel is keen to prove that, whatever his age and however long he has been out of work, he can do worthwhile and profitable work. He is determined to get away from the dole. He gives himself one year to learn the craft, and hopes to earn a living in the second year.

Nigel doesn't have the money to pay for courses, so he joins a local writers' group to find out how other writers managed to break into print.

## Joan

Recently retired, Joan enjoys gardening and needlecraft. Because of her natural curiosity she knows everything that's going on in the village – and what she doesn't know, she always finds out. Her friends call her a 'finder-outer'.

Joan likes the intellectual stimulation of interviewing people and writing, and has had a few articles published. She gets a big thrill out of seeing her work in print and would like it to happen more often, but she is easily distracted and never seems to have the time for writing. She has enrolled for an adult education centre course in Writing to Get Published, mostly because she wants to socialise with people who share her hobby, and to be 'pushed' to write more regularly.

## PRACTICAL ASSIGNMENTS

1. How far do you want to get as a freelance journalist? Will you be satisfied with the occasional published article, or are you aiming to become semi-professional, or even a full-time freelance writer?

2. How much time can you devote to journalism every week? Be realistic. Decide which days or hours of the week you will set aside for journalism. Tell your family about it.

3. Develop your personal five-year plan.

4. In addition to this book, do you want to get other forms of journalistic training? Are there any writers' groups or writing classes in your area? Do you have the time, or the money, to attend them? Which form of tuition is most sensible for you?

# 2

---

## Finding Out What Editors Want

Most freelances are surprised that editors are initially more interested in the idea for a feature than in the style in which it will be written. The explanation is simple: editors use freelances because they have fresh ideas, background knowledge, and access to information or contacts which the editors don't have.

Freelance features are valued for their content, not their style. An experienced subeditor can correct minor grammatical errors or a clumsy style within a few minutes. But no staff journalist can write the Marriage to a Belly Dancer feature as vividly and competently as the freelance whose brother is married to a professional performer.

### KNOWING WHICH FEATURE IDEAS SELL – AND TO WHOM

You know that you can write. Your features are well structured, and thoroughly researched and topical. Your creative writing tutor encourages you to send them out. Yet all they bring in is a note saying 'The editor has read with interest . . . but regrets.'

What's wrong? There are three possible reasons:

1.  You are sending your work to the wrong publications.

2.  You are writing about the wrong subjects.

3.  You are approaching your features from the wrong angle.

### DOING MARKET RESEARCH STEP BY STEP

Ninety-five per cent of all articles are being rejected because they are not suitable for the newspaper or magazine to which they were sent. This means that in ninety-five out of one hundred cases the writers could have saved themselves a lot of time and frustration by reading the publication before sending their manuscripts out.

Beginners develop an article idea first, then write the article, then send it to a magazine and hope for the best.

Professionals decide first about the magazine for which they want to write, then they analyse the publication and its readers, then they develop the idea and suggest it to the editor, and finally, they write the article.

Beginners send their work to the magazines they can see at their newsagents – with the result that a small number of national magazines are flooded with manuscripts.

Professionals write for specialist publications which are often known to insiders only, and which are constantly looking for competent writers.

## Where to find your market

How many newspapers and magazines can you find on your local newsagent's shelves? One hundred? Two hundred? All of them are, of course, prospective markets. But the most likely markets are those which you don't see at the average newsagents.

Have a look at either the *Writers' Handbook* or *Writers' and Artists' Yearbook*. Each lists publications which use freelance material, complete with editor's name, address, and basic information about what material is being accepted; for example, 'Articles of relevance to small farmers about livestock and crops; items relating to the countryside considered'. Sometimes they even include the usual rate of pay.

Another useful reference work is *1000 Markets for Freelance Writers*. It is aimed specifically at the freelance journalist and describes magazines and their requirements in more depth than the other two books. Unfortunately it is not updated frequently.

Even better are *Benn's Media Directory* and *Willings Press Guide*. Both have separate volumes for the UK and for Europe, and list around twenty thousand publications. The information is targeted at people in the advertising industry, but journalists worth their salt can derive more from advertising information than from any other data. From the precise definition of the readership, for example 'All amateur and serious photographers', or 'Cosmetics, perfumery and toiletries buyers within multiple and independent chemists, relevant department stores and counter assistants', it is easy to decide if you can write for that publication, and if so, you can write your article with these readers in mind.

You don't have to buy these books when you set out to become a writer. Most public libraries have either the *Writers' and Artists' Yearbook* or the *Writers' Handbook*, and either *Benn's Media Directory* or *Willings Press Guide* in stock. However, once you're past the 'hobby writer' phase and serious about earning money from your writing, these books are an excellent investment.

## Analysing your markets

Read at least one issue of a magazine to get the flavour before you develop an article idea for it. Then study at least two recent issues in depth before you submit your article, or approach the editor with an idea. Each time you consider writing for a publication, go through the checklists Publication Analysis (Fig. 3, page 24) and Readership Profile (Fig. 4, page 25). You can photocopy the checklists and fill them in.

## Keeping the cost down

Market research can be expensive, especially if you have to buy several issues of many publications, and perhaps their main competitors as well, to study the difference in style and approach.

Particularly with glossy monthlies and trade magazines, costs add up quickly – and there is no guarantee that an eventual sale will cover the expenses.

However, there is no need to buy every magazine which might, or might not, be a market for you, from the newsagents. Here are some alternatives:

- Many charity shops sell second-hand magazines. They may not include the titles you were after originally, and they may not be the latest issues, but they are cheap. At 5p or 10p per copy you can probably afford to buy all the issues of a year or two and study the publication in depth.

- Ask all your friends and relatives not to bin any newspaper or magazine before you've seen it. You'll quickly build up a collection of titles of which you had not even heard. Some of them are better markets than the obvious titles on the newsagent's shelves.

- Your reference library has a stock of magazines and newspapers for you to read free. Most librarians are happy to dig out past copies for you. If the publication of your choice is not included, it's always worth asking for it. Librarians try to buy the publications which are demanded by their readers.

- Libraries regularly discard their old stock, usually after a year. Back copies are sold to regular buyers. You can obtain a subscription to your favourite magazine for 50p instead of £5 per issue. Editorial requirements don't change radically within a year.

- Libraries discard their out-of-date reference books, too. The bigger

# Publication Analysis

for (name of publication):

| Address: | Contacts (names and positions) |
|---|---|
| Frequency (eg, monthly:) | Rates paid (if known) |
| Average words per feature: | Average words per sentence: |

How many of the articles in the sample issue could I have written? Which?

Is there an article to which I could add extra information, or a new angle?

How many articles are freelance written (that is, with byline of people not listed in the masthead)?

Which subject or subject group dominates the magazine (for example, fashion, health)?

Which subject group dominates the letters page of the current issue? (The editor will respond quickly to readers' requests and buy articles on those subjects)

Does the editor's comment column mention a change in editorial policy (always a great chance for new writers)?

Fig. 3. Publication analysis form.

# Readership Profile

for (name of publication):

| | |
|---|---|
| Male/female? | **Room for picture of typical reader (cut out from editorial or advertising pages)** |
| Average age: | |
| Marital status: | |
| Typical level of education: | |
| Any children? If yes: how many? Age group? | |

Reader's (or family's) annual income:

Description of accommodation:

| | |
|---|---|
| Hobbies: | Job/profession: |

What are the reader's main problems?

If I was having tea with the typical reader, what would we talk about?

Which of my hobbies or professional interests are of interest to the reader?

If I was appointed editor of this publication, what would I do to make it essential reading for the typical reader?

Fig. 4. Readership profile form.

the libraries are, the sooner they replace books. Ask your librarian. You can buy last year's issues of the two volumes of *Willings Press Guide* or the three volumes of *Benn's Media Directory* for around £10 – new, they would cost about £150.

● When sending out your query letter, ask the editor for 'back issues and damaged copies'. This works most of the time. Every editorial department has some shabby-looking back issues with missing pages lying around which sooner or later end up in the bin. Frequently, publishers miscalculate the exact amount of copies required for a particular issue, and the cupboards spill over with unwanted copies.

● To obtain a free up-to-date issue, write to the distribution department asking for a sample of the magazine. Publishers are always keen to oblige a prospective subscriber.

## TEST: CAN YOU SENSE A GOOD STORY?

Try a little test: what would you make from this information?

*Back in the days of the steam railway, the Redhill Railway brought prosperity to Little Redhampton. In 1952 it was no longer considered profitable and closed down, despite protests from Little Redhampton's citizens. In 1993 Rosalind Roundmouth, retired schoolteacher from Little Redhampton, bought what was left of the tracks and grounds. A newly founded organisation – The Redhill Railway Revival Club – raised funds to contribute towards the purchasing price. Under the guidance of a retired car mechanic, the Redhill Railway Revival Club rebuilt the line between Little Redhampton and Darkoak Green, and restored badly damaged engines. The railway opened in 1998 as a new tourist attraction. The interest from both locals and tourists has exceeded expectations by far. It appears that the new Redhill Railway is soon going to become a profitable enterprise. Its first anniversary is approaching.*

Take ten minutes to jot down all feature ideas which come to your mind. Don't read on before you've done this exercise.
 The possible ideas can be arranged in five main groups.

1.  The history of the Redhill Railway. Little Redhampton in the time of the Redhill Railway. The history of the steam railway, etc.

2.  Why it is important to revive Redhill Railway. Why we need more
    courageous citizens like Rosalind Roundmouth. Why Redhill
    Railway never should have closed down. Why we have to preserve
    our local heritage.

3.  How the engines and carriages were restored. How to repair
    badly damaged historical engines. Technical difficulties in re-
    using old tracks. Case study of how one particular train is being
    restored.

4.  The business side of the enterprise. Promotion strategies for the
    Redhill Railway venture. Finance and calculation of the venture.
    How to get a bank loan for a seemingly hopeless business venture.
    How to make money by re-opening historical monuments and rail-
    ways.

5.  A personality profile of initiator Rosalind Roundmouth. A person-
    ality profile of the car mechanic who was responsible for the
    restoration of the engines.

Tick the group (or groups) of subjects to which your ideas belong, then
decide which of your feature ideas you would tackle first, before reading
on.

Most freelance writers would go for number 1 and number 2. Most
editors want number 5! Some editors, depending on the type of publication, will select number 3 or number 4.

This gap between supply and demand accounts for many rejections.
Most editors receive piles of submission on 'The history of. . .' and opinion features, for which they have little use, but they rarely get enough
material of the sort they really want.

If you switch to the following subjects, your number of acceptances
will multiply immediately.

**Personality profiles**
Each time you read a news article or hear about an interesting event, ask
yourself: who is the woman or man behind this? Why did they do it?
How did they achieve it? What obstacles did they have to overcome?
What effects does this event have on their lives? Interview them, and
base your feature on this interview. Personalities need not be famous, but
they have to be interesting. Don't structure a personality profile like a
CV; concentrate on recent and current events. Remember that quotes
characterise a person better than descriptions.

## Features on royalty

True, the chances that Prince Charles agrees to an interview with you and reveals all about his love-life are small, but with a bit of thought you'll come up with feature ideas which can be linked with royalty. When I was editing a local paper, a freelance offered a feature about a local artist who had been commissioned to paint the Queen's racehorses. I accepted immediately. The writer was a beginner – but she certainly had journalistic instinct!

## Anything to do with sex

There is no better way to increase a magazine's sales than sex in the headlines! Editors are well aware of it, but are concerned about the standards of their magazines. Pornography is the last thing they want.

Help them in their dilemma. Find a respectable subject related to sex, and give it a very sexy title.

In women's magazines, health, beauty, love, marriage, family planning, sports and children are legitimate frames for sex articles. It should not be difficult to come up with a number of ideas: Better Skin Through Better Sex, Sexually Transmitted Diseases. Or try How to Create a Really Sexy Bedroom. Travel articles often investigate the sex lives of women abroad. Many women's magazines publish interviews with strippers, male escorts or brothel managers.

Even trade magazines won't shy back from a 'sexy' connection, provided there is a real link with their subject.

The list of possible feature subjects, ranging from The Effects of Consumer Advertising in Sex Magazines to How Male Employees are Sexually Harassed by Female Bosses, is endless. It is up to you to come up with the right ideas – and don't forget, they must be respectable! Sex in the headlines helps sell a publication. Find a respectful way which suits the publication's style of including the subject in your feature.

## Human interest stories

It is in our human nature to enjoy a bit of gossip, to find out how other people live and to form our opinion about them. True stories are much in demand by local newspapers and women's magazines. True stories must be true, and most magazines will insist on taking photos and using real names. Don't confuse them with first person 'confessions' which are often written by fiction writers.

Think of all the amazing things which have happened in your neighbourhood or family. The dog which returned after having been missing for five days. The baby which the doctors thought had died in the mother's body but was born and is perfectly healthy. The secretary who lost her job, received four hundred rejections to her application letters and, just when she was about to give up hope, was headhunted for a prestigious PA job in Paris. The aunt who bought a painting at a car boot sale for 60p and found out it was worth £3,000.

The ideal human interest story is about ordinary people with whom the readers identify, people who experience problems which could happen to the readers and who in the end, through luck or through their own determination, overcome a dreadful fate. This type of feature is called a 'tot' (triumph over tragedy).

## WRITING WITH THE READER IN MIND

When you write for a magazine or newspaper, imagine that you are writing for one person only: the typical reader of that publication.

Of course, every magazine is read by a wide section of the population. But if you can condense all these readers into an average person, you'll be able to write just for that person. This way, you'll automatically hit the right subject, angle, tone and writing style. Here are some examples:

The average reader of *What Personal Computer* is male, 30–40 years old, interested in PCs which help him run his business, and he reads the publication to find out how to get them to work more efficiently. *PC Magazine*, on the other hand, is aimed at people who make computer purchase decisions in working/business environments.

The typical *Chat* reader is a 25–40-year-old lower middle class housewife with one child and a part-time job. She spends much of her time reading magazines and watching television, and enjoys doing competitions. Another women's magazine, *Good Housekeeping*, targets women in their forties who belong to the middle and upper classes, who have a strong sense of home and family, and like cooking, entertaining and travelling.

*Active Life* is written mostly for the energetic upper middle class female over 50. *Here's Health* readers are mostly middle and upper class females over 34, interested in alternative healthcare.

The *Kent and Sussex Courier* is read by the whole community, yet the editorial team writes with a typical reader in mind: a 35-year-old secretary from Tunbridge Wells.

The editor of *Steam Classic* knows that his magazine is most popular with 40-year-old men, who are married and have a family, and who are enthusiastic about locomotives.

*Practical Fishkeeping* has an upper middle class male, aged 34, as its typical reader. Another hobby magazine, *Stamp Lover*, targets men aged

40 upwards, who belong to a middle to upper social group and who are interested in all aspects of philately. *Popular Crafts Magazine*, on the other hand, is aimed mostly at women aged 25 upwards, who belong to a middle income group, who are creative and interested in home and crafts.

## Working with reader profiles

When you write an article for a particular newspaper or magazine, write a description of the average reader on a piece of paper. You can use the reader profile form (Figure 4 on page 25) to get you started.

If you prefer, you can write the information about the average reader informally. Be as specific as you can about the reader. You can say 'she's a woman between 25 and 55'. But it's better if you are more specific: 'she's a part-time secretary, 45 years old, with three grown-up children'.

Look at Figures 5 and 6. They show reader profiles compiled by some of the students of my writing class. Defining Mr or Ms Average Reader can be fun.

Keep all the reader profiles you have collected in a notebook or folder. You will refer to them frequently.

You can even cut out a picture of someone who fits this description from an old magazine (probably the one for which you want to write). Pin them both up on the wall over your desk, or tape them to your computer screen. Look at your reader while you are writing for her.

Of course, magazines and newspapers are read by people in different age groups and from different backgrounds; but by slanting the publication at the average reader the editor makes it successful. Every editor knows who her average reader is: if you write for this reader, you win the editor's approval.

## MAKING FREELANCE JOURNALISM RECESSION-PROOF

Many editors find they have to run a magazine on a drastically reduced budget and are at the same time being urged by the publisher to develop a better editorial concept to win back readers! What type of freelance feature do they need?

Newspapers and magazines – hobby magazines in particular – are among the first items the average consumer will give up if she is short of money. Only business and finance magazines are flourishing, probably because they advise readers on how to increase their income.

If only the editors of the average women's or leisure interest magazines could find a way to present their publication as a profitable investment!

**'Downs Country' reader profile:**

The average reader is a 58-year-old gentleman called Henry, who is married to Maggie, who also reads the magazine avidly. He is round shouldered, and likes to wear tweeds or a waxed jacket and dog-tooth checked flat cap.

He lives in a semi-detached house on the outskirts of Lewes, but would prefer to own a historic cottage full of character, beams and inglenooks. Both he and Maggie enjoy gardening, and find the garden of their semi far too small.

Henry is popular and friendly, an environmentalist who takes an active interest in wildlife and nature. He takes frequent walks with his wife and their two dogs (a retriever called Ascot and a labrador called Barnaby), and always abides by countryside rules, keeping a beady eye out for litter or those who may be dropping any.

He took early retirement as a teacher at a secondary school, and is well educated and well read, with a good general knowledge of various subjects.

His wife toys with the idea of studying for an Open University degree, but never gets round to enrolling. There is always so much else to be done.

Henry likes to do a bit of fishing, but may exaggerate about his catch. He has also tried water colour painting of wildlife and landscapes.

Henry's favourite meal is traditional roast beef and Yorkshire pudding, followed by treacle sponge and custard.

He likes to partake of the odd pint, normally 'Trimbles Gut Rumbler Special' and he likes to reminisce about his young and carefree days.

He drives a second-hand Volvo with the radio tuned permanently to Classic FM. For the last ten years, he has been toying with the idea of buying a Land Rover, but he can't justify this to Maggie who says you don't need a Land Rover to drives in Lewes. He likes to use the word 'preposterous' whenever the opportunity arises.

Henry and Maggie's children have their own careers and families, and to Henry's frustration they don't share his values. He is particularly annoyed that the grandchildren are brought up on the Internet instead of in fresh country air. But when the young families visit, he tries to enjoy their companionship without quarrelling, for peace's sake.

His clothes are bought by his wife at Marks & Spencer, usually for Christmas. He reads the *Telegraph* and supports the RSPCA. On television, he watches David Attenborough's nature films and *The Antiques Roadshow*.

His political views are liberal, although in the pub he pretends to be conservative like most of his neighbours, and he admits that Tony Blair's New Labour government hasn't led to the disaster he, Henry, had predicted.

He worries about his children and grandchildren but wouldn't admit the scale of his worries to them. He gets annoyed by cruelty to animals, people who dump litter in the landscape, and plans to build a bypass close to where he lives.

Fig. 5. Sample readership profile (1).

**'Woman' reader profile:**

The average reader of this weekly magazine is a 35-year-old married woman with two school-age children. She has a good secondary education and works part-time at a building society to fit in with school hours. Her husband works in a machine shop, and they are a middle income family which means they have little spare money. They are buying a small three-bedroomed mock tudor house on an estate in Crawley. It has a small lawned back garden with little room for anything else. She has little interest in gardening but does help her husband with the decorating. She doesn't knit or sew. What little spare time she has when not running the children to various activities she spends relaxing by watching soaps on TV. She wears high street clothes and tries to watch her weight. She is interested in articles concerning health and attends the occasional fitness class. They own a white J-reg Vauxhall 2 litre Cavalier which she mainly uses. She finds her marriage a bit stale and wishes she could spice it up a little.

Fig. 6. Sample readership profile (2).

This is your chance. The following five subject groups are extremely popular with editors and readers.

## Articles on how to save money

Every editor welcomes original articles on this subject. Slant your article at the particular readership. How to Save Money on Heating Bills could be successful with a senior citizens' magazine, How to Organise a Children's Birthday Party on a Budget, for a parenting publication. Or try:

● Cooking: A Dinner Party for Under £3 Per Person.

● Health: How to Pay Less for Dentists' Bills.

● Travel: Value for Money Family Holidays.

● Cars: How to Pay Less for That Second-Hand Car.

● Finance: Cut Your Banking Charges.

● Lifestyle: Do Your Own Furniture Repair.

● Housekeeping: How Much Can Be Saved by Switching to Supermarkets' Own Brands?

● Fashion: Dress for Less.

Have a look at Shirley Conran's book *Down with Superwoman*. It is a source of ideas on how to save money in everyday life, many of which could inspire features.

Similar features can be written for hobby and trade magazines, e.g. Where to Find Good Second-Hand Photographic Equipment.

There is only one limit to your 'how to save money' features campaign: more than ever the editors have to take the interests of their advertisers into consideration. The editor of a bridal magazine, which exists almost exclusively on the advertising revenue from the fashion industry, is unlikely to publish a feature on Make Your Own Wedding Gown and Save Money. Try not to undermine the main advertisers' interests.

## Articles on how to earn money

Do you know someone who has made a hobby into a profitable job on the side? Someone who earns money by creating dolls, repairing video cameras, painting silk ties, sewing individual lace underwear, taking wedding photos or whatever? Interview them for a human interest story. Women's magazines are looking for profiles of such people. Or turn the material into a how-to article: How to Make Money from Wedding Photography.

Consider your own – and your friends' – hobbies and the skills involved. How could these skills be utilised to earn an income?

## Articles on work and careers

How to find/keep a job, how to get a pay increase, how to become self-employed: these subjects are more topical than ever! How to Get a Rise and How to Dress for an Interview come up again and again. But it isn't enough to rephrase information from a library book. You need a fresh, original angle and an optimistic approach. Spice your article up with quotes from personnel managers. What about How to Know if Your Job is in Danger, or a feature about senior citizens who've successfully started a small business?

## Articles on how to get public money

How can individuals, groups or companies obtain public money? Which grants, scholarships, sponsorships, subsidies are available? For which-ever readership you are writing (business women, college students, teenage girls, families or senior citizens), there is public money avail-able. Find out for your readers how much is available for whom, where they can get further information, and what they can do to be one step ahead of other applicants! Sources of money (and of information on how to get it) are large companies, borough councils, the national govern-ment, the EU, the UN, etc. This sector has hardly been discovered by freelances yet. The trick here is to write up the bureaucratic information in a lively, popular style.

## Articles on 'little luxuries'

Marketing people have always claimed that certain 'little luxury' sectors are booming in a recession. These include apparently unnecessary items such as take-away food, frozen desserts and wines from the supermarket. Surprising? Not at all. People are going out less, and enjoying themselves at home instead!

Base your feature on this idea: A Chinese Evening at Home (based on a take-away meal); or Dinner for Two in the Comfort of Your Home.

Another industry sector particularly successful in recessionary times is video hire. It is cheaper, and perhaps more fun, for a group of people to gather in somebody's home and watch a film together, than to go to the cinema. Smart freelances will use this trend to sell a feature, e.g. How to Organise a Video Evening for Your Friends, covering the selection of the right film(s), suggestions for food and drinks, atmosphere, who to invite and estimated costs.

## WHAT THE EDITORS SAY

Some editors give useful tips about what they do and do not want:

- Charles Donavan, features assistant, *Woman & Home*: 'The reason why we use so little of what's sent in on spec is that the writer has clearly not looked at the magazine, and made no effort at all to adhere to our style, wordcount, etc. We get endless autobiographical pieces which we don't want, and articles on anything to do with children, which we don't use either. We would welcome contributions to our human interest section called *New Direction*.'

- Frank Westworth, editor, *Classic Bike Guide* and other special interest publications: 'I edit motorcycle titles. I receive many, many, many unsolicited manuscripts about Me and my Motorbike, featuring me and My Opinions And What My Mate Bill Thinks Too. No one wants to read them, unless the author happens to be Jimi or John Lennon reincarnate. But there is something I'd like to get: features about heroic undertakings, fascinating and original insights...really good, involving writing.'

- Mick Whitworth, deputy editor, *The Grocer*: 'Some people seem to be writing for the business press circa 1948. We get a steady stream of reminiscences, anecdotes and "comment" pieces that show no understanding of the scale of our market or the content of our magazine. We operate in an industry whose total turnover is around £100 billion, yet we are offered features on vintage postcards that feature comic grocers. We are not a parish magazine.'

- Stephen Garnett, deputy editor, *Evergreen*: 'Study the magazine and write something that would suit a particular regular feature of our magazine. We get too many articles on familiar writers – Hardy, Dickens, etc – and we would like more about lesser known writers. We like articles on people's memories, but we receive too many about Christmas, 'washing-day' and other well-worn subjects. We would welcome submissions for the slots *Evergreen Melodies* (stories about singers and songs from the Twenties to the Fifties), *Cinemagic* (about old films and stars), as well as features on old radio programmes, and early TV stars and programmes.'

- Rob Keenan, features editor, *Amateur Gardening*: 'Many contributions are too anecdotal, with not enough substance. Features must be aimed at experienced gardeners, and tell them something new about gardening. The more original the subject, the better the chance of the feature being accepted.'

- Amanda Griffin, editor, *Stationery Trade News*: 'I get too many items that are written for end-users. My magazine is trade only. It is a trade newspaper for the UK office products industry, read by stationers, office products dealers, manufacturers, distributors and wholesalers. I would like more features which offer in-depth analysis of office products market trends.'

- John T. Wilson, editor, *Great Ideas*: 'I would like more features with a practical angle, experience-based, about money-making, small-scale, business ideas.'

- Brian Lund, editor, *Picture Postcard Monthly*: 'I don't want articles on a theme with a few common illustrations. I want articles which offer original research on illustrators or publishers.'

## PRACTICAL ASSIGNMENTS

These exercises will make you think like an editor, and if you understand your customers, you are half-way there.

1. Obtain a weekly women's magazine, such as *Take a Break*, *Bella*, *Best*, *That's Life*. Study it in depth until you feel that you know the average reader well, with all her problems and interests. Imagine sharing a cup of tea and a chat with her. What would you talk about? Jot your ideas down.

2. Imagine you're the editor for a week, and you are planning the next issue. Go through the magazine, page by page, look at the headlines, and at how long the articles are. Now make a list of article headlines for *your* issue, and how many words these articles will have.

3. Obtain a hobby magazine, and again study it in depth. Write a profile of the typical reader.

4. Imagine you're the editor of the hobby magazine – and plan a future issue.

5. You may like to repeat these exercises with other publications, such as your local newspaper, a daily national newspaper, a trade magazine you read at work. You can even use the time when you are waiting at the doctor's, dentist's or hairdresser's to analyse the magazines there.

# 3

## Writing the Irresistible Query Letter

Imagine you are being bombarded with unwanted mailshots. Day after day you find leaflets on double glazing, life insurance, garden furniture and antiques auctions in your post. Do you read them all? Most of them will go straight into the bin.

A week later, the garden furniture salesman phones and demands an explanation for why you have not decided yet whether to buy the set of garden chairs. You have never had a garden. Annoying, isn't it? What a waste of your time and patience.

You wish you could stop the flood of unwanted offers somehow, perhaps with a sign at your door saying 'Strictly no unsolicited material'.

This is exactly how editors feel when they receive a dozen or more unsolicited manuscripts every day. They have not asked for them, and they simply don't want them.

### QUERY FIRST

Editorial staff look at every manuscript they receive, but they don't have time to read them from beginning to end. After all, they have a magazine or newspaper to produce. Reading freelance manuscripts is a very minor part of an editor's job. It is usually left until there is time for it (and there never is). In the end it is often a secretary or trainee who sorts out the slush pile and returns at least the obvious rejections.

The editor has a quick look to see if the subject and angle of any of the remaining manuscripts are interesting and useful to her publications. In most cases, they are as useful as the brochure on garden furniture in your post if you don't have a garden. The freelances have wasted their time.

Every editor likes to be approached in a different way. Most feature editors prefer a query letter with synopsis, which is so much quicker to read than a whole manuscript.

Please don't phone: your phone call is bound to come at a moment when everyone in the editorial department is desperately trying to get the final pages ready for print! Of course, there are always exceptions to the rule. If you know that a particular editor prefers phone calls, or if the

# Nigel Nickeling, Journalist

**1, Abcde Lane
Fghijkl Town YY1 1ZZ
Tel (0000) 0000**

Doreen Dorian,
Editor 'You and Your House'

15 July 199x

Dear Doreen Dorian,

I am a regular reader of You and Your House. As a qualified mechanic and experienced DIY enthusiast, I have come up with some ideas for your magazine. I used to write technical instructions for a household appliances firm and can explain technical matters in plain English. Would you be interested in the following:

1. How to prevent costly plumbing disasters. Step by step instructions on how to prepare your plumbing system for the winter. What to do if disaster strikes (frozen pipes etc), with a 'what if' checklist. Targeted at the reader who knows little or nothing about the subject.

2. How to make your home burglar-proof. Ten clever ways to keep burglars out, costing little or nothing. Did you know, for example, that fifty per cent of all burglars break in through the ground floor back windows? It can cost as little as £5 to fit these windows with locks. With brief comments by a senior crime prevention officer and 'did you know' facts in a box.

3. How to save money on heating bills. You can reduce your household heating costs by up to 50%. Twenty ideas how to keep those costs down this winter, each with clear 'how-to'-instructions and approximate costs.

SAE enclosed. I look forward to hearing from you.

Yours sincerely

*Nigel Nickeling*

Nigel Nickeling

Fig. 7. Query letter (1).

subject is topical, then ring them, but don't waste their time. Be clear in your mind about the feature you want to write, and how you would develop it, before you phone.

## PLANNING THE CONTENTS OF THE QUERY

The type of query letter to which most editors respond favourably contains the following information:

1. The subject, as precisely as possible. Many freelances make the mistake of suggesting a subject in too general terms. For example, don't offer a feature on Belly Dancing, but on How to Become a Professional Belly Dancer, or How Belly Dance Can Help Slimming, or The World's Oldest Belly Dancers.

2. The angle. For example, personality profile of Nefertiti Osiris who is a professional performer, or advice for enthusiastic amateurs.

3. The style. For example, humorous, informative, light-hearted, factual, scientific.

4. The contacts who will be quoted. Their names, positions and, if appropriate, their relationship to you, such as 'Sheharazad Humperdinck, my sister-in-law, who has been a professional performer for eleven years'.

5. The suggested length, e.g.: 900–1000 words.

6. The author's qualifications to write on the subject, for instance: 'I am a member of the Midlands Arabic Dance Network and have been teaching belly dancing for five years.'

7. The expected payment. Remember you are offering a service – like the double-glazing sales person who dropped the leaflet into the letterbox. State your price. The editor won't take this for greed. On the contrary, it shows that they are dealing with a professional! If unsure how much to ask, write 'At your usual rates', or give a wide range such as 'My usual rates are between £30 and £110 per 1000 words.'

If the editor doesn't like the subject offered in the query letter, the freelance has not wasted much time. If the editor likes it, he or she can ask for alterations, such as a different angle or length.

Cathy Clever, Freelance Journalist
'Scribbles', 11 Abc Drive, Xyzzyx 1YW WYA,
Tel & Fax: (0000) 0000
Member of the Society of Women Writers and Journalists

Sabrina Sunday, Features Editor
Suzanne Magazine

15 July 199x

Dear Ms Sunday,

Are you interested in a feature on what it is like to be the husband of a belly dancer? How does a man feel when his wife dances in a night-club, or gives 'bellygram' shows at private parties? Does he mind when she gets fan mail from men who describe her dance as 'the most erotic, most exotic, most exciting' performance they have ever seen?

My brother, Stan Humperdinck, is in this situation. His wife, Sarah, dances professionally under the stage name Sheharazad. Stan acts as Sarah's agent, manager and accountant, and accompanies her to every show. He enjoys her success. It rarely happens, but there are occasions when he steps in if an eager admirer wants to do more than just watch!

I am familiar with the subject of belly dancing: I have been teaching oriental dancing at the local adult education centre for ten years.

I propose a 700 word feature with strong human interest and lots of quotes, and a 200 word fact file on belly dancing (as a boxed item), with payment at your usual rates. Sarah and Stan are willing to be photographed.

I enclose a stamped addressed envelope and I look forward to hearing from you.

Yours sincerely,

*Cathy Clever*

Fig. 8. Query letter (2).

The best query letters, however, are the ones which contain two, three, five, ten, twenty feature suggestions!

## SAVING TIME

Suggestion lists are great time savers for the editor. They also show that the freelance has studied the publication, is interested in the subject and could become a regular contributor. All editors prefer regular contributors to one-off submissions, because it reduces the administrative work involved.

The editor can select the most suitable ideas and write a quick letter: 'Please send nos 3, 8, 13 and 16 on spec.'

## DEAR EDITOR

How do you address an editor whose name you don't know? 'Dear Sir' is old-fashioned and will not endear you to a female editor. 'Dear Sir or Madam', 'Dear Madams and Sirs' and 'Dear Editor' are all acceptable.

It is, though, always worth finding out the editor's name, either by looking it up in the publication, or with a quick phone call. 'Dear Mr Smith' is correct, and 'Dear John Smith' is being used more and more frequently. 'Dear John', of course, is not acceptable until the editor has started signing his letters to you with 'Yours, John'.

When you get a reply from another member of the editorial staff, for example the features editor or the editorial assistant, it is a good idea to address your future letters to them directly.

### Enclosing samples and SAEs

Query letters, as well as unsolicited manuscripts, must be accompanied by a stamped addressed envelope (sae). If you are sending something the magazine staff haven't asked for, you cannot expect them to pay for the return postage. However, if an article has been commissioned, or if the editor expressed an interest in your work and has asked to see it 'on spec', you don't need to enclose an sae.

It is fine to send a stamped, addressed 're-use envelopes' label instead of an envelope if you want to help the environment and keep costs down. Much-used, much-licked envelopes are not acceptable.

Don't send samples of previously published work at this stage. They only increase the height of the pile and the editor's unwillingness to look at it. Again, there are exceptions, and if you know that an editor likes to see published work, photocopy a couple of articles which are similar in style or content to the one you want to write.

18 August 199x

Dear Ms Clever,

Thanks for your letter of 15 July. I am pleased to commission you to write the proposed feature about the belly dancer and her husband.

However, the overall length must not exceed 700 words, which must include a short boxed item. Please keep your sentences short and punchy. Can you include a mention how she got involved with belly dancing?

We need a selection of photographs (slides), showing Sheharazad during a show (if possible with fans), and at home with her husband. We will probably use two slides, but our picture editor would appreciate if you could submit at least ten.

The feature will probably be published in next year's March issue. Please send the manuscript no later than 30 September 199x. Our rates are £200 per 1000 words, plus £30 per published photo.

Please phone me or the editorial assistant, Julie Jiller, if you have any questions.

Yours sincerely

*Sabrina Sunday*
Sabrina Sunday
Features Editor

Suzanne Magazine Publishing. Ksf jdkjfdfj Akf, Bxxjdfjs Cdf jdfjksdjfds, 11 Ddfjskdf Efgh, Gfd sdkjf  EC1 1CE, Asdfdjsf Bdjfksdf Cdkf , Djfjsdkf Edkf Fds Gdsjfkd 0101010101, Hfdsjf ldfjs Jkdfs  Lkfsdskdjf  Telephone (00000) 000000, Telefax (00000) 0000

Fig. 9. Commissioning letter.

## When not to query

There are some types of articles for which most editors prefer to receive the manuscript without a preliminary query:

● News items. If something is so topical that it will be out of date in a couple of weeks, you should not waste time querying.

● Short fillers and anecdotes. Many magazines publish mini articles under headings such as 'Aren't Men Daft', 'Gardening Tips' or 'Health File'. These are often only a couple of sentences long. It would be silly to send a query letter that's longer than the article.

● Readers' letters, and comments about previously published articles.

● Travel articles in some of the national newspapers (but most magazine editors prefer queries for travel articles).

## GETTING COMMISSIONED

An editor who likes a feature idea will either commission you, or ask you to submit it on speculation (on spec). If you receive a go-ahead from an editor, make sure you know whether it is a commission.

If you are commissioned to write an article, it means that the editor promises to buy it and to pay for it. Editors tend to commission only writers who are well known, or who have contributed previously to the publication.

You need a letter confirming the agreement, including subject, deadline and price. If the editor commissions you over the phone, you can send a confirmation letter. See example on page 44.

Of course, once you are established as a journalist you will try to get as much commissioned work as possible, and only occasionally send your work out on spec.

## SUBMITTING ON SPEC

In most cases the editor asks you to submit a feature on spec. Treat this as a sales opportunity, but don't regard it as an agreed sale. There is no guarantee that the editor will buy an article she has asked to see, but your chances are increased by about 500 per cent! You know that the editor is interested. Now your success depends on how well you write the article, and if you deliver the promise contained in your query.

# Nigel Nickeling, Journalist

**1, Abcde Lane**
**Fghijkl Town YY1 1ZZ**
**Tel (0000) 0000**

Doreen Dorian,
Editor 'You and Your House'

15 August 199x

Dear Doreen Dorian,

Thank you for your phone call, commissioning me to write the article 'How to make your home burglarproof'.

I am happy to confirm that you will have the article by 10 September latest, complete with the requested colour photo for illustration. You agreed to pay £50 for the 800 word article and £20 for the photo.

Yours sincerely

*Nigel Nickeling*
Nigel Nickeling

Fig. 10. Confirmation letter.

As you become more experienced as a journalist, and the editors get to know your work, you should try to get more commissioned work instead of submitting on spec.

## WILL THEY STEAL MY IDEA?

Fears that the editor could steal a good idea suggested in a query letter are common among beginners, but totally unfounded. It may happen that an editor rejects a feature because she has accepted a manuscript on a similar subject a week before, and then the freelance is under the impression that her idea has been copied.

But editors never steal ideas. Why should they? The freelance who has come up with the suggestion is always the best person to write the feature, because she is involved and motivated.

## OBTAINING GUIDELINES

Some magazine editors have produced helpful guidelines for potential contributors, which are available from the editorial departments if you send a stamped addressed envelope.

They may include preferred subjects and angles, a description of the average reader, desired length of the piece, and how the editor prefers to be approached.

I've always created detailed guidelines for the contributors to any of the publications I edited – from the glossy German fashion magazine *Hochzeit*, the local Kent newspaper *News in Focus*, the international trade magazines *European Frozen Food Buyer* and *European Drinks Buyer*, the belly dance newsletter *Taqasim*, the Mongolian women's magazine *Ezegtei* and many others. I was always pleased to send these guidelines to potential contributors – but I was angry when the would-be journalists ignored my instructions.

Many other editors have prepared similar guidelines, for example, for *Woman Alive* and for *The New Internationalist*. If guidelines are available, this is usually stated somewhere in the magazine. Many other editors don't believe in guidelines. They state categorically that if contributors study a couple of issues, they get all the information needed.

## WHAT THE EDITORS SAY

- John T. Wilson, editor, *Great Ideas*: 'I prefer a written query letter – and don't forget the sae.'

**Starsheet**

Dear Writer,

We have read, with interest, your article/short story/letter/idea. We regret that we are not able to use it. We wish you best of luck in placing your work elsewhere.

Yours sincerely

The Editor

Starsheet Publications. Ksf jdkjfdlj Akf, Bxxjdljs Cdf jdfjksdjlds, 11 Ddljskdf Efgh, Gfd sdkjf EC1 1CE, Asdfdjsf Bdjlksdf Cdkf, Djfjsdkf Edkf Fds Gdsjfkd 0101010101, Hfdsjf ldljs Jkdfs Kkdjfs Lkfsdskdjf,Telephone (00000) 000000, Telefax (00000) 000000

Fig. 11. Rejection slip.

17 September 199x

Dear Cathy,

I have enjoyed reading your article, "Ten Tips for Travelling with a Handicapped Child'. I plan to include it in the December issue, and pay our usual rate of £20 per 1000 words, on publication.

I would be interested in a series of articles, 'Ten Tips for ' each covering a different aspect of travelling. For example, travelling with a baby, travelling with a pet, etc., one per issue. The articles must be informative, and they can be humorous. If you are interested, could you please send some suggestions?

Yours sincerely

*Toby*

Toby Tinkerton
Editor

Newsletter Publishing, 11 Aksjfsdj Bskdjfkds, D dkfkdsf Rkjfium, Ekjdfu  Acureure, Yuidfnsd,f, Udtnb 000000000, Wsdjfmvdrewec Tskdjr,
Tel. (00000)  00000,Fax (00000) 000000

Fig. 12. Letter of acceptance.

- Amanda Griffin, editor, *Stationery Trade News*: 'Send your suggestions in the form of a written query letter, or contact me by e-mail: EditorSTN@aol.com.'

- Rob Keenan, features editor, *Amateur Gardening*: 'I prefer to see the completed manuscript on spec.'

- Charles Donavan, features assistant, *Woman & Home*: 'Written query letters, please.'

- Frank Westworth, editor, *Classic Bike Guide*: 'I prefer a written synopsis with sample illustrations. I will never commission someone without reading at least one complete feature, however.'

- Stephen Garnett, deputy editor, *Evergreen*: 'The completed manuscript.'

## PRACTICAL ASSIGNMENTS

1. Find a magazine which has guidelines for contributors. You can find this information in *1000 Markets For Freelance Writers*, or inside the magazine. Send a stamped addressed envelope to the editorial office, requesting guidelines.

2. Write query letters, outlining suitable feature ideas, for at least three different magazines. These can be the magazines you have studied as part of your Chapter 2 assignments. Model your suggestions closely on already published articles, and aim them at the average reader. Remember to enclose a stamped addressed envelope.

# 4

## Breaking into Print – Step by Step

### BUILDING YOUR PORTFOLIO

At the beginning of your career it is important that you get articles published. It does not matter what and where at this stage, or if you get paid. Once you have had articles published, you can mention in your query letters 'I've had articles on this subject published in the local press', or 'I'm a regular contributor to *Belly Dancer*', which shows that you are not a beginner. It also enables you to send samples of published work should an editor want to see them.

### Your clippings book

Buy yourself a clippings book as soon as you've had the first snippet published, and use it. Don't leave your published articles lying around – you are going to lose them!

Spiral-bound clippings books are more useful than those which are glued or stapled and can't be closed properly when a lot of clippings have been inserted. Ringbinders with A4 plastic pockets are practical, because you can rearrange the order of the sheets or take them out for photocopying. Choose something in A4 size or larger. The decorative books used for personal diaries are too small when it comes to magazine articles.

A portfolio of your published work is wonderfully motivating. Browsing through your own successes will cheer you up when you're feeling low after a period of rejection slips. And it will impress your friends and visitors, too.

### WRITING READERS' LETTERS

A readers' letter is quick and easy to write, and easier to get published, if you know how to do it. Aim at publications which have a low circulation. A special interest or club newsletter with 300 readers, or a free local newspaper with a circulation of 70,000, receive far fewer readers' letters than a magazine like *Woman* with a circulation of around 700,000.

If you belong to a club or society which has its own newsletter, you know what interests or moves other members. Put forward a new idea, make suggestions for improvements, contradict what the writer of an article in the last issue has said.

Local newspapers are a great market for readers' letters. Send them a letter every week until they publish one!

Look around you, listen to what people are talking about at the post office, at the hairdressers, at parents' evenings at the school. Which are the local issues that you, or they, feel strongly about? Can you offer a new perspective, a new angle? Positive suggestions about how to deal with problems are always welcome. Don't be afraid to be controversial, or to present a view opposed to what everyone else seems to think. Local newspaper editors are happy to provide reading material which makes their readers think and talk.

### How to write it

A readers' letter is not a school essay, where you first state everything which supports one view, then everything which supports the other and weigh them up in the last paragraph for a well-balanced summary. State your view and stick to it.

Keep your letter short. Two or three hundred words are enough for a local paper. Put your main statement in the first paragraph, then add the arguments and reasons, with the most important ones first. Subeditors at local papers like to use readers' letters as fillers, and if a letter can't be squeezed into the available space they'll chop off the end.

The readers' letters which have the best chance of getting published are those which have a strong local flavour and a touch of humour. In summer, local papers receive fewer letters than in winter.

Readers' letters aren't usually paid for – although the best published letter in some magazines wins a food hamper or a pen – but they are a great way of building up a portfolio of published work.

Take your success with readers' letters seriously. It proves that you have a journalistic mind, that you can understand what interests the readers and what editors want, and that you are able to write and structure a piece well enough for a publication to print it.

### WRITING FOR CLUB NEWSLETTERS, SCHOOL AND COLLEGE MAGAZINES

Are you ready to try your hand at articles and features? Think small, and write about what you know. Do you belong to a club, society or organisation which has its own newsletter or magazine? Such publications are often put together by volunteers who are glad of extra input.

Avoid moody 'think-pieces'. Put yourself in the position of the reader. What do you want to find in your newsletter? Subject related news and information! Write short articles which give the reader interesting information about what's going on, how to achieve better results with their hobby and so on.

Club newsletters usually don't offer payment, but they are generous with bylines.

## CONTRIBUTING TO YOUR LOCAL PAPER

Local newspapers have to be run on smaller and smaller budgets. One reporter has to investigate and write about the same area which, ten or twenty years ago, was covered by five reporters.

If an aspiring journalist offers to supply local news stories free of charge, the editor will probably jump at the chance. However, this applies only to contributors who know what articles are needed and can write them well.

Hopeful writers who supply piles of poems about primroses in spring, extracts from their unpublished memoirs and praises of the uncle's shop are a nuisance. Every local newspaper editor is hassled by these ineffective time-wasters, and will assume that you belong to that category until you prove the opposite.

### Submitting news

Short news articles of about 200–300 words, with a strong local flavour, human interest and an upbeat mood are most in demand. If a teenager in the neighbourhood has won a scholarship for Cambridge University, or departs with Operation Raleigh for adventures in the Amazon jungle, or if your neighbour is a runner-up in a national businesswoman-of-the-year award, it's worth writing about.

Write it up quickly, putting the basic facts in the first paragraph, add a couple of quotes and further information, and hand it in at the newspaper office. Enclose a note saying that the editor can use the article if the editorial space is available, and that you don't expect to be paid.

If you can enclose a photo for illustration, so much the better. But if getting photos developed means delaying submission of the article until it is no longer 'news', it's better to hand it in without a picture.

Don't be disappointed if not all your articles are being used. Sometimes newspapers have more news articles than editorial space, and give preference to staff-written ones. In other weeks the subeditors are hard pressed to find enough copy to fill the column, and they will gladly use your material.

## Taking your chance in the 'silly season'

Have you noticed that, in certain months, photos are often blown up to a size which is in no proportion to their importance? This is because nothing newsworthy has happened and the subeditors don't have enough articles to fill the space. Every publication has its own 'silly season', when the silliest story is taken up and developed into a big article just to fill the space. For local newspapers this tends to happen in January, July and August.

This is your chance. Keep your eyes and ears open, and write an article about what is happening!

In the 'silly season' there is also a chance of getting a real feature in the local paper. This is usually based on an interview with a local person who does something unusual or interesting. (See Chapter 6: Structuring and Writing the Feature.)

## How to become a village or club correspondent

Most local newspapers have special pages for 'village news' and 'club news'. This is because the readers are interested in who is the new chair of the Women's Institute or where the Horticultural Society is going for its next outing – but only if they are members of the group, or if the news refers to their own village. This type of news is therefore listed under the name of the relevant club or village.

Club correspondents are usually the press officers of the local clubs. Why not join a couple of clubs? They will probably be only too pleased to have you as a press officer, especially if you have already had a few pieces published.

Some newspapers cannot afford a reporter in every village, but don't want to miss out on the local news. Either they encourage their readers to send in news – which is an unreliable method – or they find a correspondent in each village. Let your newspaper editor know that you are an available correspondent if he ever needs one in your village!

The ideal village correspondent lives in the village, is well known by the residents, is lively and popular, and involved in local groups and events. He must have a telephone, so that neighbours can ring with news and the editor can ring with queries.

A village correspondent is expected to write three to five news items of one or two hundred words for each issue, and is paid about £8 per issue. Not a lot – but this is your first step towards real, paid-for journalism!

What do you write about? Subjects are not hard to find. Mrs Smith has won the tenth prize in a poetry competition; the Scouts are looking for a new leader; the horticultural society changes the venue for its monthly meetings; the camera club invites new members.

Subeditors often despair at the offerings of village correspondents. Their articles are too wordy, and they write lengthy intros before getting to the point. Flowery phrases and words such as 'lovely', 'delightful', are loved by the correspondents, but not by the subeditors who have to cut them out.

Keep your sentences simple and active. Write only about what interests your readers. They like to hear who talked about what, but not necessarily that the chairperson in a pea-green dress delivered a vote of thanks to the speaker who wore a purple hat.

**Ten reasons to become a village correspondent**

1.  You can fill your **clippings book.**

2.  Your **social life** becomes more interesting; you are a welcome guest at many events.

3.  Your neighbours will approach you with **information** which you can use for articles for other papers.

4.  You learn **interviewing skills.**

5.  You acquire basic telephone liaison and research **skills.**

6.  You learn how to present copy and how to follow a **house style.**

7.  You get used to working to a tight **deadline** and to produce work under time pressure.

8.  You are a 'real' journalist and **get paid** for your work.

9.  The editor of your local newspaper gets to know **your name.**

10. Sometimes you are given free in-house journalistic **training.** Whenever the newspaper runs training sessions on writing style, libel or photography, ask if you can attend.

**CASE STUDIES**

**Matt**

After submitting a few short articles on amateur sports, of which the local newspaper published several, Matt offered to do some sports reporting. The sports editor of the local newspaper was delighted. 'Hurrah – here is someone who volunteers to attend sports events at weekends!'

For Matt, who spends much of his spare time watching football matches anyway, this occupation is more fun than work. The sports editor has no budget to pay Matt, but he gives him some useful tips on how to write about sports events without using clichés. On average, Matt writes one or two sports articles per week and his portfolio builds up quickly.

## Cathy

When the local newspaper advertised for a new village correspondent – the previous one had moved – Cathy rang and offered her services. To her surprise, she was taken on immediately. She was the sort of person the editor wanted: a local who knew everyone. Through her children she is well connected with the local schools, and her occasional secretarial work has put her in touch with small local businesses. Every week Cathy's column is published, together with the byline and photograph, and once a month she gets a cheque. She has become a local celebrity who is welcome at every meeting.

She also approached the entertainments editor and offered to review theatre performances for children. 'This is great. I can take the children with me and need not find a babysitter. They love it, and their comments help me write the review. And, of course, we get free press tickets. I could not afford to take them to the theatre otherwise. We look forward to the Christmas panto season!'

One of the schools has asked her if she would like to contribute to a school newsletter, perhaps even edit it: another opportunity to fill her clippings book.

## Nigel

Angry about delayed roadworks, Nigel wrote a letter to the local paper, which was published the following week. Encouraged by this success, he posted a letter every week. Several were published. One day the deputy editor rang him: 'We really like your letters, but we can't print them all. We must give space to other people as well.'

Nigel had the presence of mind to reply: 'I appreciate that. Would you like some news articles instead?' But when the deputy editor said: 'Why, what do you have in mind?' he was lost for ideas. However, he is now brainstorming for article ideas to suggest.

## Joan

A member of the local Women's Institute and Horticultural Society, Joan offered these groups her services as a press officer. To her delight the local paper has published each of her press releases in the clubs and groups section. Many of them were drastically shortened, however. 'I realised that they did not want 800 words about a meeting, and wrote shorter, more concise articles.'

Joan is now considering joining the local ramblers' group. She has heard their chairperson mention that they need more publicity.


## JOINING THE EDITORIAL TEAM

Most professional freelance journalists have one big advantage: they have inside knowledge of the publishing world. It is amazing how many of them, however briefly, have worked in a publishing environment, as staff journalists, reporters, subeditors, secretaries at a literary agency, editorial assistants, desktop publishing operators, proofreaders and so on.

This experience gives them an understanding of how magazines and newspapers are put together, how editors think and how manuscripts should be presented.

If you can spare a week or more, why not join your local newspaper for editorial work experience? Especially in summer, when many of the staff journalists are away on holiday, the editor may welcome help.

You could argue that unpaid work is labour exploitation, but from hands-on experience in an editorial office you will probably learn more than from a journalism course, for which you would have to pay a lot of money. And you are not taking away anybody's job, are you?

Practical experience in an editorial office gives you the edge over other freelances. You learn how an editor's mind works and a newspaper or magazine is put together. In addition, you can add a lot of articles to your portfolio of published work. You can also mention in query letters to other publications that you have experience in working for so-and-so newspapers – you don't have to mention that it was only for a couple of weeks!

Of course you have to convince the editor that, if he decides to take you on, you will be an asset to the office and not a bother. Editorial offices are frantically busy and staff will not have much time to look after you.

You can also apply for work experience placements with national newspapers or magazines, but these are more difficult to obtain.

## CASE STUDIES

### Matt

'It was easy to get a placement with the local newspaper because they had published my articles before. However, nobody had the time to explain a lot. I took the initiative and phoned up local charities, asking if they had any news, and turned the information into little articles. Most of these were published in the next issue.

'During my three weeks I answered the phone for the editorial team and did telephone interviews. I was also allowed to shadow one of the senior reporters. We went to the same events together, wrote separate articles and compared the results. He said I did well for a beginner, but I think I still have a lot to learn.'

### Cathy

'I couldn't possibly leave my children on their own for a whole week, but my husband agreed to take a day off work and look after them. I wrote to one of the big national women's magazines and asked if I could spend a day in the editorial office. To my surprise, they agreed immediately.

'In the morning I helped the editorial assistants with the filing. We cut out articles from other magazines and sorted them by subject, so that whenever the editor decided to do a feature on a particular subject they had some information at hand.

'In the afternoon I worked for the commissioning editor. I sent out rejection slips to would-be contributors. What a feeling! I was astonished to see how many unsolicited manuscripts they had, and most of it was clearly unsuitable for a women's magazine. One writer had sent a whole collection of children's stories, although the magazine has never published anything for children!

'I also sent out cheques to regular contributors and updated their files. This was a real eye-opener. Some of them get £600 for a single article! I wouldn't mind earning that much.'

### Nigel

'I found a one-week's placement with a drinks trade magazine. They gave me a huge pile of recent press releases, all about new products, and asked me to phone the producers to obtain additional information. I had to find out the launch date, the retail price, the quantity, the regional availability and the target consumer. I also had to ask for a photo and get a suitable quote from a senior person.

'I was talking to some pretty high-up people, and in many cases the producers were based in another country. Then I wrote them all up for the new products section of the magazine.

'One of my interviewees invited me to a press reception to introduce a new brand of sparkling wine. He had no idea I was only a work experience person! The editor laughed, and said I should go, as long as I came back with an interesting interview and did not expect to get paid for it.

'I went, just for the fun of it. We journalists were treated like royalty, wined and dined at a first class restaurant. Of course I didn't let on that I was a beginner! I listened in to one of the drinks journalists interviewing the marketing director about the label and design, and I asked some questions about their marketing strategies.

'At the end of the party I had more than enough material for an article. They even gave every journalist a press pack with photos and information about the company, as well as two bottles of the wine to sample at home.'

### Joan

'I wrote to several magazines and got no reply. Then suddenly the fashion editor of a women's magazine phoned: they were doing a photo shoot the next day and would I like to stand in for her assistant who had been taken ill?

'They were taking photos of bridal gowns in the park-like grounds of a luxurious hotel. I found myself ironing hooped petticoats, making coffee, and selecting the accessories to go with the gowns. I took detailed notes of which dresses, accessories and cosmetics were used for which photo. We spent about two hours on each photo, and the whole shoot took two days.

'The next week the fashion editor invited me to the editorial office to help select the best pictures. There were hundreds of almost identical slides of each shot. We checked for unwanted shadows, for creases in the fabric of the gowns, for facial expression.

'Best of all, I was allowed to write the captions for this photo shoot! I was so excited when the magazine came out in print. The pages are now in my portfolio, and when people look at it, they say "What – you write for THEM?" which makes me really proud.'

### PRACTICAL ASSIGNMENTS

1. Gather all the newsletters you receive. These may include your parish magazine, your Neighbourhood Watch news sheet, a club newsletter, a student publication from your college. Write a readers' letter to one of them.

2. Write a news article aimed at your local newspaper, about something that's happening in your neighbourhood or in your club. Deliver it while it's still newsworthy.

3. Could you gain some work experience? How much time could you invest? Contact your local newspaper or a magazine publishing house in your area.

4. If you have some time to spare, ask if your club would like some help with their newsletter, or if they could use your services as a press officer.

# 5

## Interviewing with Confidence

### FINDING INTERVIEWEES

#### From neighbour's daughter to VIP

You can find interviewees living in your neighbourhood, or take their names and phone numbers from press releases. You may read a snippet about someone in a newspaper and decide it is worth expanding into a magazine feature.

Interviewees don't necessarily have to be famous. Anyone who does anything which could interest other people is worth interviewing. Many freelance journalists say that they could write at least one article about every new person they meet!

So who do you interview? Start with those close to you. Your sister, who is personnel manager for a large local company, about which job skills and qualifications are more in demand. Your brother-in-law, who works for a bank, about how to approach a bank manager for a loan. Your neighbour's daughter who has just won a local disco beauty contest. The author of a book which is to be launched soon and for which the publisher has sent you a press release. The rock group which consists of three students from the local college who've got a contract for their first single from a record company.

### ARRANGING THE INTERVIEW

If you know the people personally, you can just ask them when you meet them next. Most 'normal' people are flattered to be interviewed; tell them honestly that you cannot guarantee publication.

Don't say you want to write an article about *them*. Say that you want to write about their work, their hobby, their charity, etc. Everyone enjoys talking about their work, but few like to talk about their private lives.

If potential interviewees are suggested by a press release, ring them up. They will probably ask for which publication you write. Mention the newspapers or magazines which have published your work before, and also to which editor you will be sending the interview. You must appear confident!

**Cathy Clever, Freelance Journalist**
'Scribbles', 1 1 Abc Drive, Xyzzyx 1 YW WYA,
Tel & Fax: (0000) 0000
Member of the Society of Women Writers and Journalists

1 October 199x

Dear Amanda Amour,

I am a freelance journalist, writing for several newspapers and magazines. I am also a great fan of your films!

The press officer of Andromeda Films, André Anderson, has sent me a press release regarding your latest film, 'Autumn Affair'. I wonder if you would like to meet me for an interview.

Sabrina Sunday, the features editor of Suzanne Magazine, is interested in publishing it. I enclose a feature which has been published recently by the same magazine, to give you an idea of my writing.

The issues I would like to discuss are the different characters you represent in this and in your last film, how you prepare for a particular role, and how you enjoyed filming in Britain after three films made in Hollywood.

As you can see from my address, I live in your area, and could meet you either in your home or at any other place you suggest. I look forward to hearing from you.

Yours sincerely,

*Cathy Clever*

Cathy Clever

Fig. 13. Request for an interview.

If you want to approach a VIP who has never heard of you, send a letter to him, or his agent or manager. They are unlikely to agree to be interviewed unless you can say that a particular editor has expressed interest, or unless you have had similar interviews published. (See Fig. 13, page 60.)

Your written request for an interview should suggest a date, a meeting place, the subject you want to talk about and the publication(s) for which the feature is intended.

You should give them a rough idea of the subjects you want to discuss during the interview, but avoid revealing the precise questions in advance otherwise you will end up with boring answers, carefully phrased by the public relations department.

## When, where and how

The interviewee's office or home is the ideal meeting place. People are more relaxed in familiar surroundings.

It is tempting if an interviewee suggests meeting at a luxurious restaurant, especially if they offer to foot the bill. Once I interviewed a manager of an exclusive Swiss restaurant chain. But have you ever tried eating, talking and taking notes at the same time? While I tried to handle knife, fork and pen simultaneously, the delicious food got cold. And all I could hear when I played back the recorded tape was the noise of cutlery.

## PREPARING FOR THE INTERVIEW

You don't need to be an expert on the chosen subject to make your interview a success. Experts who interview experts often lose touch with the uninformed reader's curiosity.

Ideally, you should know as little or as much as the typical reader of the magazine. If you interview a crime prevention officer for a women's magazine, you don't need any special knowledge. It does not matter if your questions are simple and naive – they are exactly the questions the readers want to ask!

Of course, the situation is different if you want to interview him for a police staff magazine. In this case you should know something about the subject, or your questions will seem naive.

It is vital that you establish yourself as a competent journalist. Wearing a suit will boost your confidence and create a professional atmosphere.

Have a list of questions ready when you go to the interview, arranged in the order you want to *ask* them. The order in which you want to write them up is irrelevant at this stage.

## Using notebooks and tape recorders

A tape recorder is the most reliable recording method. It encourages the interviewee to talk faster and more spontaneously than if you take notes, and they cannot deny having said certain things afterwards! However, it can take up to eight hours to transcribe a one-hour recording.

Note-pads are convenient when it comes to writing up: paragraphs can be highlighted, cut out, rearranged, but unless your shorthand is fast you will lose details from the interview. I take notes of important comments and refer to the tape for detail.

## HOW TO START AND HOW TO FINISH

The minutes before the actual interview are the most embarrassing; you will both feel better once the interview has started. Get straight into it, without chats about the weather.

Your interviewee's time – and yours – is precious. A well-prepared interview of 30 minutes provides ample material for a 1000-word feature. One hour should be the maximum if you have several markets in mind.

If your interviewee is nervous, put them at ease by asking simple questions which show that you appreciate what they are doing. Begin with a subject you know they enjoy talking about.

## INTRODUCING INTERVIEWING TECHNIQUES

### From gentle to cruel

Experienced journalists start with 'harmless' questions until the interviewee feels relaxed and safe. The critical subjects come later. One unwelcome question at the beginning may ruin the interview.

### How to get the quotes you want

If you don't understand an answer, it is better to ask immediately than to phone up afterwards for clarification.

Questions about well-known facts are unwelcome. Imagine what the famous actress will think of the journalist who asks, 'In which films have you played?'. Try 'Which film did you enjoy most? Why?'

If you agree with your interviewee's opinion, resist the temptation to say, 'Yes, I understand'. I have made this mistake, and realised afterwards that he would have continued talking if I had kept my mouth shut. I lost exactly *the* quote which I had been after.

Ask them for their opinions on everything. The stronger their views are, the better. These quotes will make your feature come alive.

Asking 'open questions' which cannot be answered with 'yes' or 'no' results in spontaneous answers which make splendid personality feature material. 'What were your impressions of filming in Paris?' invites a better answer than 'Did you like filming in Paris?'

Don't ever mention your own opinion. If you agree with your interviewee, the interview gets boring; if you disagree, you spoil the atmosphere, and either way you are wasting precious time.

Be flexible about an unexpected turn of story; some of your question ideas may turn out to be a dead end, while your journalist's instinct will suggest new angles.

## COPING WITH FAMOUS, SHY OR DIFFICULT INTERVIEWEES

Most interviewees are helpful, proud to be interviewed or eager to impress the media.

If your interviewee is giving evasive answers in flowery words, he would prefer certain things not to come to light. Here is your story! Simply repeat the question, phrased differently, until he talks.

Some interviewees ask questions to test your knowledge and possibly undermine your self-confidence. Simply ignore them, even if you know an answer, and continue. You are the journalist, you ask and they answer.

Others give exciting information, adding 'But don't publish this.' You are not allowed to use any 'off the record' information. Say that you will respect their request, and keep your promise.

However, some interviewees make everything they tell you 'off the record', which means you cannot get enough information and quotes for a good feature. This can be because they are insecure, or because they want to appear mysterious and important. In this case you say: 'OK, if you have nothing to say to our readers, there is no point in me interviewing you.' They will become more helpful immediately!

Occasionally an interviewee tries to dictate the answers word by word, including full stop and semicolon. Who do they think you are? The shorthand typist? Simply put away pen and pad, lean back comfortably in your chair and give them a wide smile. They will quickly treat you as a journalist!

## TAKING PHOTOS

If you want to take photos do it after the interview, when the interviewee is relaxed and animated. Or take a photographer with you who can capture your interviewee in animated conversation, with gestures, facial expressions, etc. and a photo captioned 'Actress Amanda Amour in discussion with journalist Cathy Clever'.

## WRITING IT UP

Write the interview up soon, while you can still read your shorthand and your impressions are fresh. You will not be able to use all the interesting information you have, at least not in one article. Concentrate on one aspect for each publication.

It is alright to shorten answers, restructure sentences, drop repetitions, correct the grammar and rephrase certain answers so that they read better. However, don't be tempted to change the tiniest bit of the meaning, or you will be in deep trouble.

Most interviewees ask to see the feature before it goes into print. They will show it to their family, friends or PR consultants who will change everything completely. If they insist, offer to read it out to them on the telephone. They can then correct obvious misunderstandings, without a chance to consult anyone.

## TELEPHONE INTERVIEWS

Once you are familiar with the basic interviewing techniques, you can conduct most interviews by telephone. This saves you a lot of travelling time and cost. Agree in advance a mutually convenient time, and also who will be phoning whom. Have a list of questions ready.

## INTERVIEWS BY POST

These work well if it is not possible to meet the interviewees in person or to make telephone contact; for example, if you are interviewing a missionary in deepest Africa.

Interviews by post are also a time-saving device if you want to ask several people the same questions. Phrase your questions so that your interviewees can answer them in just a few sentences. Most of your questions must be 'open', otherwise your interviewees will simply say 'yes' or 'no' and you won't get any quotes. Photocopy the questionnaire, write a covering letter explaining the purpose of the survey, and give the date by which you need the reply and enclose a stamped addressed envelope. (See sample covering letter, Fig. 14, page 66 and sample questionnaire, Fig. 15, page 67.)

Not everyone responds. You will probably get around four replies for every ten questionnaires.

A drawback of this method is that some interviewees reply in long, complicated sentences which don't read like natural talk, and others supply quotes which read like extracts from their sales literature.

## PRACTICAL ASSIGNMENTS

1.  To practise interviewing skills before you go out on a 'real' interview, ask a friend if he or she can spare you an hour to talk about their hobby. Remember to take detailed notes of what they say. Don't rely on 'knowing it already anyway' or 'surely I'll remember this'.

2.  Make a list of people around you, who have interesting hobbies, jobs or experiences.

3.  Do some market research. Find at least two possible publications for each subject. You may want to look at the newsagents, or consult directories such as *Willings*, *Benn's*, or the *Writers' and Artists' Yearbook*.

4.  For your first 'real' interview, choose either a local person who has just done something remarkable (returned from an assignment as a volunteer development worker in India, won a regional beauty contest, had their first book published), or someone who shares your hobby and is particularly skilled or experienced at it.

    Ask the questions the reader of your local newspaper or of your hobby club newsletter would like to ask.

5.  Write up this interview, and submit it.

6.  Now it's the time to query some of the other markets with your ideas for interview features. Editors want interviews.

**Cathy Clever, Freelance Journalist**
'Scribbles', 1 1 Abc Drive, Xyzzyx 1 YW WYA,
Tel & Fax: (0000) 0000
Member of the Society of Women Writers and Journalists

1 September 199x

Dear Madam or Sir,

I have been commissioned by Suzanne Magazine to write an article about male au pairs. Can you kindly assist me with my research by answering some or all of the questions in the enclosed questionnaire.

I am working to a tight deadline and would appreciate your reply by 10 October.

Publication is scheduled for spring next year, and I will send you a photocopy of the published article.

Thanks for your help. SAE enclosed.

Yours sincerely,

*Cathy Clever*

Fig. 14. Request for an interview by post.

### Cathy Clever, Freelance Journalist
'Scribbles', 1 1 Abc Drive, Xyzzyx 1 YW WYA,
Tel & Fax: (0000) 0000
Member of the Society of Women Writers and Journalists

QUESTIONNAIRE

1. Do you accept male applicants for au pair jobs? If yes, do you think it is easier (or more difficult) for them to find a placement than for female au pairs? Why?

2. Do you get requests from families specifically for male au pairs? If yes, can you describe the typical family which employs a male au pair, and their reasons?

3. Do male au pairs, on average, do the same type of work as female au pairs, or are there differences? Which?

4. Are, in your experience, placements of male au pairs successful?

5. Can you possibly put me in touch with a family and their male au pair, so that I can interview them and take a photo of the au pair at work?

6. Do you believe that in future there will be more male au pairs? Why?

7. Any advice you want to give to boys who want to become au pairs?

8. Any other information you want to give?

Fig. 15. Questionnaire for interview by post.

# 6

## Structuring and Writing the Feature

### RESEARCHING

Depending on the type of article, and how much you know about your subject already, your research may include:

- A visit to your library, to borrow and order books and to look up reference works. If possible, make the most economical use of your time by researching for more than one feature at a time.

- Using press releases. As soon as you have had a few articles published on their subject, most organisations and companies will be happy to send you regular free information and the latest news, as well as interview ideas and even photos. Many press releases are waffling texts written in PR style, but they are valuable for ideas and contacts. (see Fig. 16, page 70 and Fig. 17, page 71.)

- Interviewing an expert.

- Interviewing other people, who hold a different opinion or who represent a different viewpoint.

- Your own observations, for example of the local colour and atmosphere for a travel article.

### DEVELOPING IDEAS INTO ARTICLES

You know exactly what you want to write about. You have researched the subject and the possible markets. And yet, you sit at your typewriter and just don't know how to get started. Professional journalists, staff or freelance, turn out reams of copy within tight deadlines. They have developed methods of writing articles on anything, without delay.

Some of the most brilliant features in the national newspapers and magazines are structured with the experienced journalist's standard formula. Using a tried and tested approach is a good way to get started.

## USING AN INFALLIBLE FORMULA

Few journalists are willing to reveal their methods, but you can certainly try mine. Of course, you don't need to follow them strictly, and you can adjust them to suit your particular subject or market. I don't claim my guidelines are the only possible way to structure a feature, and they are not always the best. But I promise that they work, every time.

## HOW TO WRITE A 'HOW TO' ARTICLE

'How to' articles are easy to sell and easy to write. Almost any subject can make a suitable 'how to' article, and almost everyone can give competent advice on one or more subjects. Articles which show, in the widest sense, how to earn or save money are bestsellers.

Before putting pen to paper, make sure you've 'done it' yourself. Most 'how to' articles are timeless and can be reslanted and sold to several publications. Study several target markets, and note the subjects, style and length of their 'how to' articles.

Use short words and sentences, avoid wordiness at all costs. Link words such as 'and then. . .', or 'after that', are superfluous. Always give precise measurements. 'Add half a teaspoonful of salt, and simmer for three minutes' is more helpful than 'Add a little salt and simmer for a while'. Be detailed without patronising the reader. Mention prices where appropriate.

This is the typical structure:

1.  One introductory paragraph which motivates the reader.

2.  Between three and twelve **bullet points** (or up to 20 numbered paragraphs) of one or two sentences. Arrange them in chronological order (what to do first).

3.  The last paragraph should give sources of further information: further reading, addresses of mail order catalogues, courses and workshops.

Before sending out your manuscript, give it to a friend to read, to see if your instructions are clear and foolproof. If possible, ask your friend to try them out!

### Writing 'filler tips'

A shorter version of the 'how to' article is the 'tip'. Many magazines use these to fill space between articles, or they combine several tips from

# Purple Panther Productions

Press release

Embargoed until: 11 November 199x

Jazz-punk group launches single

Oakhurst-based punk band Pink Poodles are launching their first single 'Paranoid Parachute' on 1 December 199x. Track A, 'Paranoia' is a mixture of soft rock and punk rock, with strong instrumental interludes. 'Parachute' on track B is a lively punk piece with traditional jazz elements.

The members of the band, Aaron Alberti (17, sax, lyrics), Bertie 'Bad' Brummer (21, percussionist and composer), and Coralie Corrall (18, guitar, vocals) are students at Oakhurst College.

All three are available for interview. For more information, photos, a review copy of the single or to arrange an interview, phone Paola Pomms on (0000) 00000.

Fig. 16. Press release (1).

# Fran's Frozen Foods

PRESS RELEASE

11 November 199x

Fran's pizzas are the best

Fran's are the most popular brand of frozen pizzas in East Sussex, according to an independent survey carried out by Frick's Data Services in October.

98.5% of a representative sample group of consumers aged 18 - 80 named Fran's Crispy Quark Pizza as their favourite in the '6" frozen pizza with  crispy quark base and mushroom & tomato topping' category.

Product shots (b/w prints and trannies) are available. The managing director of Fran's Frozen Foods, Ms Francesca Firenze, is available for interview: Tel (000)  00000.

Fig. 17. Press release (2).

different contributors under a single headline. The market includes many weekly women's magazines and several special interest and hobby magazines.

*Chat*, for example, publishes about 15 such paragraphs under the heading Our Tips, and they pay £10 for each (plus £5 for a photo) – and if yours is the Star Tip of the week, you earn £30.

*That's Life* publishes several contributions every week for the column Tightwad Tips (ideas for money saving) and pays £20 for each – and £30 if you add a photo. This magazine also has occasional columns for tips on healthcare and other subjects.

*Amateur Gardening* also has a Tip of the Week, which earns the writer £10.

The key to success for tips is to aim them at a specific magazine. Ask yourself: what problems does the average reader have? How can I help with advice?

Writing tips is a good option for you if you lead a busy life and can't find the time for thorough research and for writing long pieces. Tips are quick to write – only about 20–70 words long. They don't need any research, since you are only sharing knowledge you have already. And they pay well – between £10 and £50 per tip. This works out at an excellent rate per 1000 words.

## WRITING THE INTERVIEW FEATURE

Personality profiles are based on interviews, and are always in demand. Bear in mind that quotes characterise a person better than description. Most beginners structure personality profiles like a CV in chronological order, which tends to be boring. Here's how to do it better.

1.  Begin with a short, succinct quote which characterises the person's attitude to his/her work.

2.  One sentence about the person, who he/she is.

3.  One sentence which quantifies his/her recent success with a precise, surprising figure ('one million records sold').

4.  One paragraph quote about how he/she feels about this achievement, broken up by a description of his/her appearance, gestures, facial expression or tone of voice ('there is pride in her deep voice when she talks about. . .').

5. Continue alternating one or two paragraphs of narration with one paragraph of quote.

6. End with a humorous quote.

## WRITING NEWS ARTICLES

The news articles must say who is doing what, where, when, how and why. Of these, the 'what' is the most important, and must be said in the first sentence. Avoid lengthy names (such as East Sussex County Council, or Citizens' Advice Bureau) in the first paragraph, because they put the reader off.

The who, what, where, when, how and why should be covered in the first two paragraphs. Many writers try to squeeze all the information into the first sentence, which results in constructions such as 'Citizens of Boarshurst are being urged by Ms Emma Louis, secretary of the local Save our River charity, to join a letter writing campaign which started last month and is intended to continue until September, by sending letters to the county council demanding in politely phrased requests that the decision to allow motor boats on our river should be reconsidered, to protect the wildlife in and around the section of the river between Boarhurst and Crannington which would be endangered by the traffic of motor boats.' Better start with: "Our river wildlife is in danger," claims Ms Emma Louis. The secretary of the Save our River charity has started a campaign to prevent motor boats between Boarshurst and Crannington.' Then arrange the facts in order of importance.

When there is not enough space on the editorial page, editors have to cut news articles. This is done at the last minute, and there is no time to discuss the matter with the journalist who wrote the piece.

However, there is an unspoken agreement throughout the world of journalism that, if in doubt, subeditors will cut from the end. Don't leave the most important item to the last paragraph; it may be chopped off!

## WRITING THE TOPICAL FEATURE

Many newspapers and magazines publish in-depth features to provide background information to news articles. The difficulty is that you have to obtain controversial quotes, and compile and verify a huge amount of information within a short time. If you can at the same time give the feature a new angle and show the facts in a different light, you deserve a byline in a national newspaper!

1.  Start with one or two sentences describing the fact as it is generally seen.

2.  One paragraph which shows the fact in a new light.

3.  One paragraph quote by someone who is competent and well-known and who sees the facts in this light.

4.  Two paragraphs analysing the background of the situation in more depth.

5.  One-paragraph quotes from someone who holds a different opinion (probably your first contact's competitor or opponent, or the 'villain').

6.  One paragraph quoting your first contact, contradicting what the second person said.

7.  One paragraph narration.

8.  One paragraph quote from a third person, such as the woman in the street.

9.  Continue by alternating one or two paragraphs of narration, one paragraph of quote. As topical features usually cover unexpected events for which the editor has not planned space in advance, she will throw another piece out and fit the topical feature instead. This means that topical features often have to be cut drastically to fit into the available space. The same rule applies as for the news article: make sure that you give the essential bits in the first few paragraphs, and the less important information further down.

10. End with a paragraph which gives a summary and a critical (but not patronising or moralising) future outlook.

## WRITING THE SUBJECT FEATURE

The typical subject feature is of a specialist nature (e.g. Hungary as a Developing Market for Ice Cream Exports), often long and in depth. Because of the wealth of information and the factual treatment, subject features tend to be boring to read. Do your best to liven them up with quotes.

1.  Begin with an **intro** paragraph which may contain your byline ('Amanda Scribble visited Hungary to investigate the country's market potential'). This paragraph must contain a surprising fact, which is topical and of relevance to your feature, to hook the reader.

2.  Begin the main text with a provocative quote from someone who is knowledgeable (perhaps the director of a company which exports ice cream to Hungary).

3.  Write two paragraphs of explanation about the situation (why do so many western European producers target the Hungarian market? How much ice cream do Hungary's own factories produce?).

4.  For the rest of the feature, alternate quotes and narration. Use quotes from several people who represent different viewpoints (another British producer eager to export, as well as the leader of a 'buy Hungarian' anti-import pressure group, a Hungarian housewife and mother of four, and an ice cream salesman).

    For narrative, use hard facts ('The most popular flavours are chocolate, coffee and coconut'), backed up with figures ('total annual ice cream consumption is 1.7 litres per capita').

5.  Keep your own opinion out. Instead, finish with a quote from someone competent who sums up the situation in the way you think, and who can give a brief statement of what to expect for the future.

## WRITING THE CONTROVERSIAL FEATURE

This one is difficult both to write and to sell. Don't tackle it until you have some experience, and even then you should discuss the approach with the editor first.

Structure a controversial article or feature like a subject feature, and make sure that you give the two opposing parties equal space, but give the last word to the party with which most of your readers identify.

As subeditors cut from the end, don't write a huge chunk about party A and then a huge chunk about party B. The subeditor who is pressed for space may cut most of B's quotes. Use a pattern of one paragraph for A, one for B, and one for facts, and repeat this until the end of the feature.

## WRITING THE OPINION FEATURE

Opinion features are the most popular category among beginner writers, but the least popular among the editors!

There are hardly any commercial outlets for opinion features, unless you are a VIP expert in your field. However, you can try writing a comment column for your club's or society's newsletter. Last but not least, the structuring recipe for opinion features is suitable for a reader's letter.

If you want to see it published, avoid the typical beginner's approach (opening with a well-known fact, with a proverb or a question) – this would read like a school essay! Avoid a patronising tone.

1. Start with a surprising fact, if possible relevant to the season or to a topical event, and develop your thoughts from there.

2. Alternate two sentences of thoughts, two sentences of facts, throughout the feature. This makes your article easily readable. Quote a couple of precise figures and state the source; they make you appear competent.

3. Finish with a question, related to the future.

## WRITING THE PERSONAL EXPERIENCE FEATURE

Never pretend to have tried something if you haven't, or your readers lose their trust in you. Take courage and try out that helicopter flight, hypnosis, or bungee jump. Mention your scare just before take-off, or how you almost changed your mind before jumping, and your readers will believe every word you say.

Start with a surprising fact or quote. Alternate narrative and quotes, facts and experience. Create atmosphere by describing noises and smells. Consider writing in the present tense for extra impact.

The best illustration is a picture of you in action, to prove that you've actually done it! Get a friend (or a professional from the newspaper's photographic department) to capture you in trance during hypnosis, or in full harness ready for the bungee jump.

## WRITING A REGULAR COLUMN

Before suggesting a column to the editor, make sure you have plenty of ideas. Imagine you are having tea with the average reader: what would you talk about? You need not represent the average reader's opinion, as long as the subject is one which interests him. Editors appreciate columnists who receive bags of fan or hate mail. To stimulate the discussion, write about dog fouling, abortion or fox hunting. You can be sure the readers will write in.

A well-written column reads as if the author had written it in a careless, chatty tone, but it requires careful phrasing. Prune your manuscript until there is no superfluous word left.

## DEVELOPING A GOOD WRITING STYLE

Every writer has her own style, and so has every magazine and newspaper, depending on the audience it wants to reach. The *Daily Mail*, for example, uses shorter sentences than *The Financial Times*.

Try to imitate the writing style of the publication for which you want to write as closely as possible. Pick out one or two typical articles and examine them closely. How many words do they use, on average, in a sentence? Out of one hundred words, how many words have more than one syllable?

### How to make a subeditor happy

- As a general rule, try to keep your sentences below 25 words, and never exceed 33. Don't use a long word where there is a short one, and prefer Anglo-Saxon words to Latin ones.

- Use lots of expressive verbs, and keep adjectives and adverbs to a minimum.

- Ruthlessly cut all the following words out of your first draft: very, really, truly, totally, completely, absolutely, rather, quite, extremely. They are unnecessary. For example: 'He was quite disappointed that he did not get the job.' Either he was disappointed or he wasn't. 'The village was totally destroyed by the earthquake.' 'The good news made her really happy.' Watch out for 'very'; many freelances use this word in every sentence. You should not use it more than twice in a thousand words.

- Never use the word 'only' in connection with a price. State how much an item costs, and let the reader decide if it's cheap or expensive.

- Avoid PR speak, especially when quoting business people and when using extracts from press releases. 'High quality' is an over-used phrase, and can be replaced by the simple word 'good'. Words such as 'unique' and 'exceptional', popular with public relations people, are out of place in journalistic writing. If you describe the product, service, place or event properly, your reader will come to the conclusion that it is 'unique' if it truly is different from all others.

- Avoid empty words, such as 'interesting', 'nice', 'lovely', 'exciting', 'fascinating' and 'beautiful'. They pretend to describe something, but they don't. Choose words which give a more accurate description instead. Beauty is in the eye of the beholder, anyway.

- Avoid exclamation marks. Ideally, each of your sentences should be powerful enough to get your point across, without exclamation marks. The weaker the writing, the stronger the temptation to use exclamation marks. Two exclamation marks in a one thousand words text are acceptable.

## Following the house style

Most publications have their own rules on grammar, spelling and the use of words. If you write regularly for a particular paper, ask for a copy of the house style notes.

These state whether it is the managing director, the Managing Director, the md, the MD, or the M.D. who gave the speech, whether Mrs Beech, Ms Beech or Diana Beech was elected, and whether she became chairman, chairwoman, chairperson or chair. They also decide the question of whether a phone number is written '(000) 000', '000 000' or '000-000'.

Not all potential questions are covered in the relevant editors' house style sheets. In this case, you must decide for yourself.

It is a good idea to set up your own house style, to which you refer whenever there is no other guidance available. This makes your writing consistent. It would look awkward if, in an article which contained lots of contact addresses, the telephone numbers were prefaced sometimes 'tel.', sometimes 'Tel:' and sometimes 'phone'.

## Avoiding sexism

The use of 'he' and 'she' worries many writers. You don't want to be sexist, but you don't want your article to read like a legal document on equal opportunities either. You have the following possibilities:

1. You can use 'he', 'his' and 'him' throughout. Example: 'If a writer wants to sell his work, he must study his markets.' This is easy to read and easy to write, but it can prevent female readers from identifying with the article. It may even offend them. Another disadvantage is that it gives your writing a conventional, even old-fashioned flavour, and you add to the subconscious belief of many people that men form the majority of people and are more important than women. Choose this form if you write mostly for a conservative, exclusively male audience.

2. You can use 'she', 'hers' and 'her' throughout. Example: 'If a writer wants to sell her work, she must study her markets.' Again, this is easy to read, but can prevent male readers from identifying and may offend them. It gives your writing a modern, even aggressive flavour. Choose this form if you write mostly for a female and feminist audience.

3. You can use 'she or he' (or 'he or she', 'she/he', 's/he' and so on) throughout. Examples: 'If a writer wants to sell her or his work, she or he must study his or her markets.' 'If a writer wants to sell his/her work, s/he must study his/her markets.' This form is certainly non-sexist and non-offensive, but it interrupts the flow and makes the article difficult to read. Choose this form if you write mostly short, factual articles.

4. You can use 'it' throughout, as some progressive writers suggest. Example: 'If a writer wants to sell its work, it must study its markets.' The idea is to abolish gender altogether, and with it any remains of sexual discrimination in writing. In practice, this doesn't work as well as in theory. For example, 'He gave it to her' becomes 'It gave it to it'. This can make it difficult for the reader to follow. Such a progressive approach would rarely endear your writing to the average editor.

5. You can use 'they', 'theirs' and 'them' throughout the article, even when referring to a single person. Example: 'If a writer wants to sell their work, they must study their market.' When this form was first introduced, some people were upset because it was grammatically wrong. However, it is short, practical, non-offensive, non-sexist, allows the text to flow and is easy to read. This has become the standard for many writers and many publications, and is becoming increasingly popular.

6.  You can use 'he' for some paragraphs and 'she' for others. This gives your writing a real-life flavour and creates an effect as if you were using case studies. Both men and women can identify with your writing, and it is easy to read. This form is used frequently in America, and is becoming popular in Britain, too. However, it only works for books, long articles and features. If you switch from one gender to another within a sentence or a paragraph, or switch five times in a two-paragraph article, the result can be ridiculous.

    I have used this approach for much of this book.

Of course, if a publication's house style requires a particular way of dealing with 'he' and 'she' then you must follow it, whatever your own house style and opinion is.


## PRACTICAL ASSIGNMENTS

1.  Make a list of subjects about which you know more than most people. Don't be modest, and don't stop until you have at least 20 ideas. If you think carefully, you will come up with many more. These don't have to be earth shattering subjects, and you don't need a master's degree. Knowledge acquired in your hobby, work and family life is a valuable source. For example: 'How to help a child with bereavement', 'How to teach your child to write', 'How to make a belly dance costume', 'How to grow herbs on the window sill', 'How to make bead jewellery', 'How to make parsnip soup', 'Coping with redundancy'. The more specific you are, the easier you will find it to compile a list. Don't just say 'gardening' but 'growing tomatoes on the balcony' and 'How to get rid of slugs'.

2.  Obtain a magazine which publishes tips. Write at least two tips for them, and send them off.

3.  Select a subject from your 'expertise' list. Study some publications which cover this subject area. Now write a practical 'how-to' type article, aimed at a specific publication, if possible modelled on a recently published article.

4.  Phone the press office of a large company or your local council, and ask them to send you their latest press releases. Study them. Does one of them contain information that could inspire a feature article? Perhaps you could interview one of the people mentioned?

5.  If you belong to an organisation, church, college or club which publishes a newsletter, consider offering them a regular column. What would be a suitable theme? How long should each article be? Should the style be chatty, serious, amusing, provocative? What subjects would you cover? When you have ideas for at least five contributions, approach the editor with your ideas and a sample.

6.  Look at some of the writing you've done earlier. Edit your own manuscripts before you send them off. Pay particular attention to the tips given under 'How to Make a Subeditor Happy' (page 77).

# 7

# Branching Out

## WRITING ADVERTISING FEATURES

Do you read the advertising features in your local newspaper? Perhaps not. You find them boring, predictable, with more flowery phrases than entertainment value or information. You don't want to read about yet another business and its 'commitment to quality', about how it 'achieves highest standards' because 'customer satisfaction' comes first for its 'friendly, helpful staff' who are 'always at hand'.

The advertisers, of course, are flattered to see themselves praised in print. They are happy if their services are described as 'delightful', 'fascinating', 'exciting', 'interesting' and 'unique'.

A good advertising feature, however, does more than flatter the advertiser. It captures the readers' attention, gains their trust, informs and entertains them. In short: it brings customers for the business.

### Attention, interest, desire, action

Do you know AIDA? Not Verdi's opera, but the formula to which skilled marketing people work. It is their recipe for a successful advertising campaign. You can apply it to creating advertising features, or advertorials as they are sometimes called.

- A stands for **attention**. You have to make the readers look at your feature, so arouse their curiosity at first sight. Most ad features fail at this point already.

  Faced with a huge choice of tempting headings on the news pages (Sex at The Bus Stop, Sonya Challenges The Football Star, Ex-Mayor Jailed), who is going to be attracted by typical adfeat headings such as Experienced and Polite Staff Are Always at Hand, and Where Quality and Customer Satisfaction Come First?

  And with all the photos of little children, cuddly dogs, TV stars and page-three girls, who is going to waste a second glance on the portrait of a middle-aged man in suit and tie?

  The average readers pick just what springs to their eye immediately, and discard the rest unread. You have only a few seconds to capture their attention.

- I for **interest**. Make your intro paragraph so interesting that they want to find out more.

- D stands for **desire**. Make them want the product. Most adfeat writers exaggerate the desirability of the product so much that the reader does not believe them, over-using PR words such as 'exciting' and 'delightful'. Be honest with your readers, and they will believe you and your recommendation.

- A is for **action**. Stimulate the readers to go and spend money on the product. Here, too, most adfeat writers go too far, pushing the readers into purchasing action. 'So on your next free evening, go and visit the Pin and Needle Restaurant. . .'.

   Your readers feel patronised if you try to force the decision on them, particularly if you say that a three course meal costs 'only £57 per head'. State the prices, but leave it to the reader to decide if it is 'only' or 'just'. What seems a reasonable price to you may be unaffordable to a single mother or an unemployed worker. 'Only £9.99' intimidates them. Allow them to relax, to form their own opinion, and they may make their own decision to go and try out the meal.

I find that most adfeat writers ignore A (attention) and I (interest), thus losing most potential customers. Then they exaggerate D (desire) and A (action), bore most of their readers and intimidate the rest.

### More than praise in print

Can you do better? Why not try your hand at an advertising feature, just to find out? Write about a friend's or neighbour's business. If you like the result, you can show it as a sample of your work to your local newspaper. Many papers have no money for freelance reporters and fiction writers, but there is almost always a budget for advertising features.

   Advertising features are also called 'advertorials', 'editorial promotion' or whatever name the advertising department has invented.

   Instead of the predictable litany of company praise, try any of the following approaches.

*Personality profile*
Base it on an interview with the owner (see page 72). This version is the easiest to write, and the most interesting to read. Give it a lot of human touch, which will make the reader remember the person (and her or his business) for months. Instead of the usual head and shoulders full-front portrait, take a photo of the person at work.

*Personal experience feature*
This means great fun during the research, and a chance to get a freebie, too. See page 76 on how to write the personal experience feature.

*Company history*
This is popular with companies celebrating an anniversary. It works well if the company is at least 100 years old, if you can use old photos and if there are plenty of anecdotes. Readers are not interested in who succeeded whom as chairman: they want to read the funny bits.

Obtain old photos from the company's archives, if possible with people. Then take your own photo of the same venue or equivalent situation. This makes eye-catching 'now' and 'then' pictures.

*Trend survey*
This is difficult to write for a beginner. Have a few questions ready: Who are your youngest customers? Your oldest? Do people of different age groups have different tastes? Do men select different products from women? Do they know what they want, or do they require advice? Which product is particularly popular with price conscious consumers? Which colour/style/size, etc. is in at present? Do couples take the decision together . . . or is it the man/the woman who decides? Photo suggestion: manager or staff demonstrating the most popular product to customers.

*Staff round-up*
Take photos of several members of staff at work. Select staff who are working at different levels and in different departments, e.g. saleswoman, receptionist, manager. Give preference to people who have been with the company for many years, and whom your readers are likely to meet. Describe their daily work, their responsibilities, and how they contribute to the finished product. Use their quotes to liven up the text.

## HOW TO WRITE A PRODUCT TEST COLUMN

You are honest and diplomatic at the same time. You enjoy trying out new things, have a vivid imagination and can use words creatively. Then writing a product test column could be your strength!

Many newspapers, trade and consumer magazines carry such columns, in which someone gives a subjective view. Products tested include, depending on the publication, everything from lipstick to cars, from wine to sports equipment, from pens to holidays.

Rates vary enormously; they can be nominal or substantial. In some cases there is no payment at all – but the 'freebies', i.e. the free products, make up for it.

Once you've decided which type of product you are going to test, you write to the press departments of the producers to request a sample. They are usually keen to have their products reviewed, but first you must convince them that you are a bona fide journalist and that your product tests will get published. Send a photocopy of your press card, of your Society of Women Writers and Journalists membership card, or whatever credentials you have. Better still, enclose a sample of a previously published product review.

The easiest way to break into product testing is possibly to write for your local paper, if necessary without payment at first. They often request a local angle for all features. You can achieve this by simply including the names of stockists in the area.

Specify precisely the product you are testing: 'mascara, waterproof, black', or 'night cream for ageing skin'. You need between three and twelve products for a proper test column.

Make sure you give each a fair trial – for example, don't test the duration of one lipstick during a theatre performance and the other during dinner or while making love! To test nail varnish apply the ten different products at the same time, one on each nail, so that they are exposed to the same amount of nail biting and washing up.

## Finding the right words

Ignore the flowery phrases of the press releases which arrive with the products. 'This exquisite moisturiser is perfectly balanced and uniquely suited for today's busy lifestyle. . .'. Find your own descriptions, based on your experience. They will necessarily be subjective, which is alright for an opinion column. Plain language is best, but you may use colourful metaphors and comparisons. Say what the product looks, smells, feels like.

Use comparisons with which your readers are familiar and which mean the same to them as they mean to you. Wine journalists, for example, tend to use words like 'biscuity' or 'hint of vegetable', and leave their readers wondering if the wine tastes of rich tea or chocolate biscuits, of broccoli or asparagus!

Be critical. If you find fault with a product, you owe it to your readers to be honest. But make sure that you say something positive as well. 'This cream had a wonderfully fresh fragrance which reminded me of peaches, but after one hour my skin felt tight and itchy.' Or: 'Despite three coatings, this nail varnish lasted only one day. But it was easy to apply and dried quickly.'

State the name of the product and the manufacturer precisely, as well as the quantity and – important – the recommended retail price.

## Accepting 'freebies'

Once you are established as a journalist in your field, especially if your writing includes product tests, you will be wooed by manufacturers and their public relations consultants.

Will you remain unbiased if a cosmetic producer sends you the whole range of autumn colours to test for your beauty column? If you are among the lucky handful of travel writers who get invited to foreign press trips, will you give the sponsoring travel organiser the same treatment as others? Be as honest as you possibly can. It is alright to:

- Accept small gifts which have no great commercial value, on such occasions as Christmas, a press reception or a product launch.

- Accept an invitation for a meal.

- Accept samples of products which help you do your research (for example, if you are a beauty columnist, a lipstick in the latest shade, or if you are a wine writer, a bottle of wine).

- Accept travel expenses to visit a factory or attend a product launch. However, it is rare for companies to offer to refund travel expenses, so don't rely on it.

- Ask for samples, free admission to theatres and exhibitions, review copies of books and records and so on if you are certain that you will write about them, and confident that you will get the article published.

- Send a thank you note to companies which have sent you samples or gifts.

- Write more about companies which have been helpful with your research and allowed you to sample their products, than about those who have even ignored your request for a brochure.

- Send photocopies of articles which mention products and services to the relevant companies.

However, you must not:

- Accept valuable gifts which have nothing to do with the subject you write about.

- Accept gifts where the quantity is out of proportion to what you are doing. For example, if you are writing a feature about champagnes, you don't need a whole case of each vintage.

- Accept anything with the promise or unspoken understanding that you will praise a product or service in return.

- Put your own interests (continuing supply of free samples) before your readers' interests (objective reporting).

- Penalise companies which don't send samples by writing negative comments about them.

- Ask for samples if you are unlikely to write about the products or services. Begging letters from false 'travel journalists' requesting free accommodation are an example.

- Accept cash (except for travel expenses).

- Sell products you are given for research.

## WRITING ABOUT TRAVEL

Many journalists dream about being a travel writer, touring the world at somebody else's expense and writing an article now and then. The market is competitive, and it's hard to make a living. Even if you find a sponsor for your trip to Florida and a newspaper to buy your articles at a rate of £100 per 1000 words, you cannot fit more than a couple of two-week trips into a month, which means you won't earn more than £200 per month.

Few journalists make a living from travel writing. Others specialise in other subjects and do occasional travel writing to finance their holidays.

### How to write a travel feature

Articles about exotic places untouched by westerners, and about your immediate neighbourhood, both sell well, provided you come up with an unusual angle. To Madrid on a tricycle? With Grandma in the Himalayas? Monte Carlo on a budget? The ideas are endless. And you don't have to travel far. Explore the charms of your home town with your notebook, and it is travel writing.

For a travel article it is alright to use the first person approach, and to tell the story of your personal experience.

Avoid boring starts ('The Spanish coast is a popular holiday destination'). Instead, start with a surprising fact, or a funny quote.

A good travel feature entertains first and informs second. Talk to the locals, and include their quotes, as well as personal anecdotes. If you can add a sprinkling of humour, so much the better. Weave the facts unobtrusively between the lines of your article, or put them into a separate box at the end of the manuscript.

Take notes while you are on location. Don't rely on your memory – you are likely to forget those small details which make up the atmosphere of the place and which will help your article to come alive. The hungry cats waiting for the return of the fishing boats, the toby jugs hanging from the ceiling beams, the smell of fried mutton. Use all your senses. Don't note just what you see, but also what you hear, smell, taste and touch. A few words about the smell of the place recreate the atmosphere better than several paragraphs about the sights.

Attention to detail is the secret of good travel writing. Don't try to cram everything you experienced on a single holiday, and all you know about one country, into a single article. Instead, write one article about a market, another one about the historical churches, yet another about the folk festival.

## Where to sell your travel writing

Travel editors are almost the only editors who, on the whole, prefer to see complete manuscripts instead of query letters, perhaps because in travel journalism writing style is more important than contents.

Model your features in length and style on those published in the magazine or newspaper you are targeting. This means, for a daily broadsheet newspaper, around 800 words. For a tabloid, only around 350. Travel magazines and inflight magazines take longer features.

Women's magazines and weekend magazines also publish travel features.

In addition, you may find that specialist magazines are hungry for travel features... as long as you cover their specialist angle.

For example, a magazine for doll's house collectors would probably be interested in your visit to a doll's house museum in China. A newspaper like *Overseas Jobs Express* could want your feature about how you worked your way around the world in one year.

Your chances of getting travel features published are increased if you can supply photos.

## WRITING REVIEWS

When reviewing a book, a play, a film or an exhibition, you should give your personal impression as well as some facts.

If it is the work of amateurs, mention as many names as possible. They will be delighted to see their names in the paper. Be generous with praise, and careful with criticism.

When you are reviewing the work of professionals, on the other hand, you can be frank. You are not obliged to recommend a play just because the theatre gave you free tickets. However, readers prefer reading positive reports. You should always mention some positive aspects as well. If you feel there is nothing positive to say whatsoever, contact your editor. He may decide to publish your piece nevertheless, or he may decide that as the subject was so terrible, it doesn't deserve a mention at all.

Read review columns by other writers and learn how they handle the delicate task of criticising. A diplomatic strategy is to say for whom the reviewed work is suitable: 'If you enjoy crude jokes, you will love this play. Those who prefer subtle humour may be disappointed.'

## CASE STUDIES

### Matt

'I'm doing test drives for the local paper, borrowing the latest cars from the local garages, and the manufacturers pay for the petrol. At first I didn't know what to write, and copied the information from the brochure, but the editor didn't like this approach.

'One Saturday I helped my mother with her shopping. She commented on how easy it was to load the shopping into the boot and to squeeze the car into the tiny parking space outside the supermarket. I quoted her. The garage manager told me that because of this article several women had come to see the car. I knew I was on the right track then.'

### Cathy

'I'm writing a test column for the local newspaper. It has become popular with readers, so the editor asked me to continue. I'm trying out products suitable for families with children. At first I wrote about products I had bought, but now I get free samples from manufacturers and shops. My husband and children enjoy the testing, and I use their comments as quotes.

'A local toy shop says that sales of reviewed products have soared.

Mind you, I've had a couple of nasty letters from manufacturers whose products were of poor quality.

'I also sent an article about our holidays, with the angle "travelling with a handicapped child" to a magazine, and it was accepted. Then I interviewed families with handicapped children about their travelling experiences, and sold the article to another magazine. I think I will specialise in this subject.'

### Nigel

'Whenever a DIY shop, a plumber or a similar business wants an advertising feature, the editor of the local newspaper calls me. I get £20 per advertising feature, plus expenses.'

### Joan

'I was sure that my travel feature about my once-in-a-lifetime trip to Tanzania would sell, but it has been rejected. Then I wrote a piece about where the BBC has made a film locally, visiting all the locations and interviewing some of the local extras, and the first editor I queried commissioned it. He said it was topical, and they didn't get enough travel pieces about places in the UK.'

## PRACTICAL ASSIGNMENTS

1.  Write a product test. Aim it either at your local newspaper, or at a hobby magazine, or a club newsletter. Try out at least three different products of the same type. This could be cars, lipsticks, face creams, frozen pizzas, tools, glue sticks, finger cymbals, or anything else you like. Test them thoroughly, and obtain additional information (source, price, etc.) about them. Then write an article that is informative as well as entertaining. Offer it to the editor for publication, with the suggestion that you could write more.

2.  Write a review. You may like to review a play, a panto, a recently published book, a television documentary, your local amateur dramatic society's annual variety show, a video, or similar. Local newspapers often welcome reviews of local evening events, as long as they are submitted quickly. Hobby magazines and club newsletters are usually keen to get reviews of recent books and videos on the subject. Offer your review for publication.

3.  Take notes for a travel article, either when you next go on a holiday, or simply take a fresh look at where you live. Make sure you get quotes.

4.  Write that travel article, aimed at a market of your choice.

# 8

## Earning More Money from Writing

### TAPPING THE BEST PAYING MARKETS

Some publications pay as little as £2.50 per 1000 words, others pay £25 or £250. A small fee can be a great reward for the hobby journalist who writes for fun, and for the beginner who is eager to build a portfolio of published work. But once you've entered phase 3 (see page 18), or are aiming towards semi-professional or professional status (phases 4 and 5), you will concentrate on those markets which offer good or excellent rates.

Of course they are more demanding than your local paper or club newsletter, but by now you are an experienced writer. You have developed the writing and marketing skills which make a good journalist. For an experienced writer, breaking into the top-paying markets is as difficult or as easy as it is for a beginner to get a letter published in the local newspaper.

You have mastered one – there's no reason why you should not succeed with the other. Below are some examples which will give you an idea.

Among the publications which pay a good fee (£50–£100 per 1000 words) are:

- The lower circulation national women's magazines, such as *Woman Alive, The Lady, Home & Country*.

- Many national magazines targeted at a specific group of society, for example, at the elderly, at the disabled, at young parents.

- Most national magazines which cover a specific hobby, such as collecting doll's houses or teddy bears, fly fishing, model making, embroidery or riding motorbikes.

- Special interest publications which have a geographically wide but narrowly defined readership, such as *Overseas Jobs Express*.

- Most of the glossy county magazines.

- Most trade magazines.

Among the top-paying publications (£100–£400 per 1000 words) are:

- National newspapers. Payment is a matter of negotiation but you can expect a fee in excess of £120/1000 words. If you are considered to be an expert in your subject, and if you have had features published in other prestigious publications, you may get up to £400/1000.

- The big circulation women's magazines. They pay around £200–£400, again depending on the writers' status.

- High circulation trade magazines offer between £100 and £250.

- Some special interest magazines, especially hobby magazines which cover an extremely popular hobby and have achieved a high circulation, are likely to pay between £100 and £250/1000 words.

- Business magazines. Aimed at executives and managers of large companies, and with a large often international circulation, they can afford to pay between £150 and £400/1000 words.

- Inflight magazines. Payment is often around £150/1000words.

Of course, a change in editor or in editorial policy can mean a change in rates of pay, and in most cases payment is 'by arrangement'. But the above examples can give you an idea of what to ask for when negotiating your fee. More publications and their rates are covered in *The Writers' and Artists' Yearbook*, *The Writer's Handbook* or *1000 Markets for Freelance Writers*.

## WRITING FOR WOMEN'S MAGAZINES

No women's magazine is exactly like the others. Although a good idea may be suitable for several of them, the treatment must be different. Editors get annoyed if writers assume that one woman is like another, and that one women's magazine is like another. Why does one woman buy *Bella*, while others buy *Seventeen* or *Marie Claire*?

The most important factor is the age group. For example, if you write a feature about people who underwent a sex change, you must choose interviewees who are the same age as the readers. For example, 18–30 for Company, and 35 upwards for *Women's Journal*.

Consider their average income, too. For a feature on how to buy a second-hand car, think carefully if you choose a Porsche or a Fiat Panda as an example.

Other considerations are whether the average reader has children, whether she has a career, and if she is more domestic or outward oriented. Remember that most women's magazines are keen to buy features which are sex- or money-oriented. Approach your subject accordingly. The major features are almost always commissioned work, but fillers are often unsolicited material. Some women's magazines state categorically 'No unsolicited manuscripts'. Don't let this put you off. It doesn't mean that they are not using freelance material at all. Send in feature suggestions instead; if the editor says 'Well, maybe. I'd like to see this feature, send it on spec' it is no longer unsolicited.

If editors think of commissioning you to write a feature, they will ask for samples of your work. Send something which is as similar to the magazine's style as possible.

## WRITING FOR TRADE AND BUSINESS MAGAZINES

The advantage of writing for trade magazines is that you have little competition. Trade magazine editors are not usually inundated with unsolicited manuscripts. They welcome contributions which are specifically aimed at their readers.

However, it can be difficult to understand the magazine's editorial requirements. If possible talk to a typical reader, for example a frozen food buyer if you want to write for *European Frozen Food Buyer*.

Study one issue in depth. Ask the editor or the distribution department to send you an out-of-date or damaged copy, or pay for a new issue. Many trade magazines have guidelines for contributors.

When I was acting editor of *European Frozen Food Buyer*, and deputy editor of *European Drinks Buyer*, I wrote detailed editorial guidelines explaining the angle, length and style I wanted. I even included suggestions for features I would like to see.

To my surprise most aspiring contributors, even after studying the guidelines, sent in pieces such as A Holiday in Iceland (perhaps she thought 'ice' was a sufficient connection with 'frozen'), and The History of Mineral Water.

Others took the guidelines seriously, and came up with several suggestions which were 'near misses'. In this case I explained where they went wrong, and asked for more ideas. Most of them became regular contributors.

Remember that trade magazines are business-oriented. The readers want to know how they can do better business, and how to save and earn more money.

Don't be discouraged if you don't know anything about frozen food, the stationery trade, window manufacture or retailing. What counts is that you are willing to take an interest in the subject.

Start by interviewing and writing about the people who are experts. After a few interviews you will be amazed how much you have learned about the subject. Of course it takes some time to get into a subject, so it is best to concentrate on one or two subjects and become an expert in them, rather than trying a bit here and a bit there.

Writing about business and finance is one of the most lucrative areas of journalism. If you are interested in business, it's worth learning about the subject, for example by reading business publications and by interviewing business people.

## Tips for interviewing business people

The first interview with a business person can be daunting, especially if you know little about the subject and fear that you might make a fool of yourself. Here are a few tips, as well as questions which are suitable for almost any type of business:

1.  Remember that you don't have to be an expert to interview an expert.

2.  When interviewees mention figures ('our sales have increased by eighteen per cent over the last year'), ask what these figures refer to. Is your interviewee talking about UK, European or worldwide sales? Is he referring to sales in volume, or sales in value? If sales have increased in volume only, the company may be making less profit than the year before; perhaps they had to reduce prices to undercut their competitors. If sales have increased in value only, the company may be selling fewer products than the year before; perhaps they simply increased their prices.

3.  Don't accept PR-speak from your interviewee. Everyone will try to tell you that their product offers 'excellent value for money' and is of the 'highest possible quality'.

4.  Ask who their target consumer is. If your interviewee claims that the product is suitable for everyone, insist on details. Every product is designed with a specific consumer in mind. Ask for the socio-economic group, the age group, the gender and so on.

5.  Ask how consumer behaviour has changed over recent years.

6.  Ask how your interviewee expects consumer behaviour and demand

for the product to develop over the next five years. He will predict increasing demand for the product. Keep asking for details.

7. Ask what influence the European Union has had on the business.

8. Ask if, and how, developments in Eastern Europe are influencing the market. Increased competition? Any plans for import, export?

## SELLING AND RE-SELLING YOUR WORK

To make the big money, you must use your research and writing time efficiently. If you sell ten different articles based on one subject, you can cut down your research time to one-tenth. This gives you the time to research, write and sell even more articles. It increases your output and your income.

### Can I sell the same article twice?

It is possible to sell a feature more than once, as long as you sold first British serial rights (FBSR) only. You can offer, for example, second British serial rights, or first Italian rights. State on your manuscript, or in the accompanying letter, where the article was published originally.

You can sell the article several times, as long as these publications are non-competing. A piece on how to become a bilingual secretary abroad, based on interviews with three enthusiastic young women, could be published in a young women's magazine, in a magazine for secretaries and PAs, in the local newspaper and again in *Overseas Jobs Express*.

Of course you will have to make changes. The young women's magazine may be interested in covering their leisure interests, whereas the secretarial magazine will want to know details about working conditions, office equipment and career prospects. *Overseas Jobs Express* readers will be interested in how they got their jobs, and the local newspaper will only want the interview with the girl who came from their area.

## SELLING ABROAD

### Think European

As the European countries co-operate more closely in more areas than ever, the need for information from and about our neighbour states is increasing rapidly. You will have noticed how much editorial space in newspapers and magazines has been dedicated to European subjects.

At the same time, readers and editors in other European countries are eager to learn about what is going on in the UK. This situation offers a great chance for freelance journalists. When I was deputy editor of a business magazine with European readership, I was often approached by editors from other countries, asking if I could recommend a freelance business journalist in Britain.

Writing for foreign markets can be very profitable. This does not mean, however, that it is easier to sell work abroad than in your own country. Editors in Sweden or Luxembourg receive the same amount of unsolicited and unwanted manuscripts as their UK counterparts.

If you want to enter a niche market in Europe, you need to know how to approach foreign editors and what type of manuscripts they really want.

Real demand exists for the following categories: business and technical features, personality features, news articles.

## Business and technical features

Many new European and worldwide publications have been launched recently. You will find their titles and addresses in *Willings Press Guide* or *Benn's Media Directory* in your reference library.

Watch out for titles beginning 'European. . .', 'Europäische. . .', etc. Most of them are specialist or trade publications, keen to find contributors outside their own country, and they are paying good rates. Technical, financial, computing and business magazines are the best paying publications.

Background knowledge in the relevant industry sector (such as advertising, food and drink, or rubber processing) is highly desirable. However, a keen interest in the subject, plus the ability to learn quickly and make contacts with knowledgeable people, is more important.

If you specialise in one subject, you will be able to write about what is going on in this sector in the UK market for a dozen publications in various European countries.

Some magazines are published in English; others are willing to sub a contributor's broken French, or to translate news articles into Spanish, provided the contents are what they want.

## Personality features

Few features editors are willing to go to the trouble of translating and publishing a feature from a foreign contributor if it could be written by one of their native, regular freelances. Most general interest and how-to features fall into this category.

However, there is considerable demand for personality features. If you have a chance to interview a VIP, who is internationally known and based in your country, regard it as potential foreign markets material. Profiles of an opera singer, a football star, or a politician can be published in five or ten different countries at once.

## News articles

Consider becoming the UK correspondent for a newspaper on the continent, particularly if you live in or near London and are interested in economic and political issues.

The biggest national dailies abroad have their own fully-staffed offices in London, but many medium-sized newspapers cannot afford a full-time journalist in every European capital. They are eager to find writers who can supply them with news and features on a regular basis. During the summer months, when very little happens in politics, the international news editors in all countries are desperate to fill their pages. Short features on environmental, social and cultural issues are welcome.

### How to approach foreign markets

In addition to checking out titles and their contents in *Willings* and *Benn's*, you can explore foreign markets by buying foreign general interest, women's and business magazines at major newsagents in the UK, although they are usually expensive.

Whatever their language, it is possible to learn from their advertisements and illustrations at which audience, age and social group they are targeted, and to see how long their features are.

Bear in mind, however, that general interest and women's magazines are less keen on foreign contributions than the specialist publications.

You can approach overseas agencies in the countries of your choice. If you are a specialist in a certain subject, perhaps environmental or religious affairs, the national news agencies such as the German DPA (Deutsche Presse-Agentur) may be interested in your news articles. To maintain the news value you have to submit them by fax.

In some countries rates for freelances are much higher than in the UK. Denmark and Sweden, for instance, are lucrative markets. Southern and Eastern European publications usually pay less.

Remember to sell British rights only to your UK publisher. Then there is nothing to stop you from enjoying a supplementary income from European publications.

### Using international syndication

If personality or travel features are your speciality, approach a **syndication** agent. Agents have contacts in many countries and may sell your features a dozen times. They charge 50 per cent of the fees you earn from them, but they pay for the postage abroad, for necessary translations and so on. You simply send them a photocopy of your published article, or of the manuscript.

Syndication agents prefer features which are of interest to readers in many countries. They don't want 'How the local government reorganisation affects East Sussex villages', but they are interested in an interview with a well-known concert pianist. Personality profiles and interview features are popular with syndication agents.

Photos help them sell your work. To persuade syndication agents to take you on, you have to convince them that you can send features in bulk – a dozen per month, if possible.

You find syndication agents, their addresses and the material they are looking for in the *Writers' and Artists' Yearbook*.

## CASE STUDIES

### Matt
'I enjoy watching motor racing. I live not far from Brands Hatch, and whenever there's an important race I try to interview as many drivers as possible. At first, I published them in the local newspaper, but then I landed some in the big magazines. Whenever a driver is known internationally I send the interview to a syndication agent, who sells it in Australia, New Zealand, Canada and other English-speaking countries. I have become their expert on motor racing.'

### Cathy
'After having a couple of features accepted on travelling with disabled children, I interviewed a blind pianist. I sold this piece to a women's magazine. On the strength of this feature I was then commissioned to write one about a disabled designer. It seems there is a market for profiles of disabled VIPs. I approached a syndication agent, who liked the articles but said he would not take me on unless I could submit at least one manuscript per week. I will approach him again in a year or so.'

### Nigel
'I'm writing for several trade magazines abroad: news, interviews, what's going on in the trade in Britain. It was difficult to get into these markets at first, but now I'm contributing regularly. Some of them pay very well, but others don't and it's difficult to chase up overdue cheques abroad. However, British editors are always impressed when they see

that my features on the same subject have been published abroad. In this way, my foreign features increase my sales in the UK.'

## Joan

'I offered a feature about women in Tanzania to the editor of a women's magazine. She phoned and asked me if I could write about their sex lives. I could not. I talked to so many women in Tanzania about so many subjects, but not about sex. Now I know. Next time I go abroad, I know what to research.'

## PRACTICAL ASSIGNMENTS

1.  Look back at your 'expertise list' (see page 80). To which hobby, business or special interest publications could you contribute? Can you think of an aspect of your work or hobby about which you know more than the average reader?

2.  Obtain some hobby, trade, business or special interest magazines. Study them carefully, then develop several ideas for articles. In which format would your articles have the best chance for which magazine?

3.  Now write query letters (see page 37).

4.  Do you have special knowledge which might appeal to magazine readers abroad? If so, find out which magazines in other countries cover the subject, and contact them.

5.  Could you write for a high circulation women's magazine, or a daily newspaper? Study them closely for feature length, angle and writing style. Then query them with your ideas.

# 9
## Building a Good Relationship with Your Editor

Most of your contact with editorial staff will be in writing, some in person and some over the phone. Whenever you meet, write or ring your editor, prepare what you want to say and try to get the right image across. Concentrate on being friendly, cheerful, helpful, professional, honest and efficient.

## PRESENTING A MANUSCRIPT

Many freelances believe that editors decide about acceptance of a manuscript according to its outer appearance. 'How to write' books and magazines create an image of editors who always have a ruler at hand, and anything with less than 1.5" margins automatically lands on the rejection pile. However, these books and magazines are usually written by freelances, who have never worked on the editorial side!

In reality, editors buy contents, not presentation.

Before you cry out in protest because your creative writing tutor has told you otherwise: yes, I have worked as a magazine and newspaper editor; yes, I have published manuscripts which arrived as hardly legible, pale print outs on flimsy, dog-eared sheets. So have many other editors, particularly on specialist publications.

Remember, however, that the reason why editors buy freelance material is to save time.

Sloppy presentation costs time during editorial production, and only a unique feature will be considered worth the trouble.

A clean, legible manuscript saves time for the subeditor and the typesetter and is greatly appreciated.

### Basic rules

The standard rules for manuscript submission are simple:

- typed (handwritten work will not even be looked at, except for readers' letters)

- double-spaced (for easy reading, corrections and changes by the editorial staff)

- margins on both sides (again for corrections; normal correspondence margins are alright)

- on white A4 paper, typed on one side only (you can use a faint tint if you wish, but avoid bright colours)

- layout kept simple (fancy logos, a variety of type fonts and varying type sizes reveal the beginner).

## Correcting errors

Keep your manuscript neat and tidy. A single typing error will not exclude your manuscript from publication, but spell-checking and proof-reading of the original manuscript is the freelance's work and it will annoy the editor if he has to do your job.

Of course you can use correction fluid and photocopies. Handwritten corrections, however, should be avoided. A single word can easily be misread by an editor or typesetter who is not familiar with your handwriting. If there are several typing errors in your manuscript, type it again.

Staple your pages firmly together, or, if the manuscript is too long to be stapled, number all pages and write the title next to each page number. Loose leaves get lost easily in the pile, and paper-clips tend to clip pages to the wrong manuscripts. It is not necessary to put your manuscript into a folder.

On top of your first page (or, if the feature runs over many pages, a cover sheet) write your name and address, the title, the type of manuscript (for example 'feature' or 'news article') and the word-count.

## Counting the words

Please don't cheat with the word-count. You may write '1000 words' if your manuscript has 995 words or 1005. But don't claim to have a 1000 words feature if you have only 800 in the hope of getting better pay, or if you have 1200, the editor's word limit for features is 1000 and you did not know how to cut. False word-counts cause trouble during editorial production and editors don't take kindly to this.

Some editors like the word 'more' at the bottom of each page, and 'ends' at the bottom of the last one.

Don't worry if you cannot find a brilliant title for your feature. The editor is likely to change it anyway if it is not short or long enough to fit

## Summer in the land of Genghis Khan
By Christine Hall
2000 words, FBSR

'I've got an overseas assignment for you, but I'm afraid it's in . . . ehm . . . Ulaanbaatar.' The BESO (British Executive Service Overseas) man's voice sounded apologetic at offering me such an out-of-the-way place, and surprised that I knew where it was. I was to help launch Mongolia's first ever women's magazine – a dream assignment for a magazine editor like me.

The library books arrived and were far from reassuring. Mostly over 50 years old, they mentioned Genghis Khan, Gobi Desert, vodka, dinosaurs, horses and nomads living in tents. The only modern book, the *Lonely Planet Survival Guide*, had worrying news. Mongolia suffered from food shortage. The only foodstuffs to be had in Mongolia, the book indicated, were mutton and flour. Flour, the author had added cautiously, was not always available. Gloomy prospects for a vegetarian!

I packed my suitcase with as much foodstuffs as I could carry, and set off. My client, Ms Baljinnyam, had worked in diplomatic service in Switzerland and spoke fluent English. She met me at the airport and immediately put me at my ease. When she heard that my heavy suitcases contained food, she broke out in laughter.

'Oh dear . . . another one who has read that *Lonely Planet* book! They all come bringing food. You won't need that here. True, a few years ago during the switch from communism to market economy there was a temporary problem, but really, we have enough food. The writer of that

Fig. 18. First page of a manuscript.

into the layout, or if it contains the same words as another heading in the same issue. However, you can help by writing several title suggestions in brackets under the initial title.

## Intros and cross-heads

You can phrase the first paragraph so that it can be used as an 'intro', that is printed in a different typeface, catching the reader's eye. Freelances are not expected to write cross-heads (small subheadings). The graphic designers and layouters insert them if and where they look good and fill a gap.

If you want a word or sentence printed in italics, underline it in your manuscript. Don't use different typefaces and sizes, and avoid fancy logos and so on.

Always put the essential information at the beginning of your feature. A production editor who has to shorten a feature always cuts the last paragraph.

You can further help by attaching a contacts list to your manuscript, with names and telephone numbers of people and organisations mentioned, in case of urgent last-minute queries.

## CHECKLIST

Before sending out the manuscript, ask yourself:

1.  Is this article of interest to the readers of the publication?

2.  Has a friend, tutor, or member of my writers' group read the article critically and suggested improvements?

3.  Have I proofread it carefully?

4.  Have I followed all the basic rules of presentation?

5.  Does the manuscript look neat and tidy?

6.  Does it contain my byline, my address and a word-count?

7.  Are the enclosures (photos with **captions**, sae) complete?

8.  Is the envelope strong enough for the manuscript?

9.  Is the postage sufficient?

10. Have I enclosed a letter suggesting further article ideas?

For submission on disk or by e-mail, see page 132.

## LOOKING AT EDITORIAL PRODUCTION

Lay people often believe that the editor accepts the manuscript and gives it to the printer. But the printer never sees the manuscript!

An accepted ms is either filed in the issue for which it has been commissioned, or held in stock for future use.

Often, editors cannot tell when they will be able to use a manuscript. How much editorial an issue contains depends on how much advertising space has been sold. The more successful the sale representatives have been, the more pages are allowed for editorial.

For technical reasons, magazine page numbers are normally multiples of eight or four. If an advertiser cancels a spread (a double page), the publisher has to cancel four pages, which means that two editorial pages have to be dropped. This may mean that your freelance feature has to be postponed to a later issue.

It can happen, however, that a one-page ad comes in at the last minute. Then the editor has to find material to fill three extra editorial pages. This is when he is glad to have good freelance material of varying length in stock. Perhaps an advertiser cancels his $1/4$-page ad, and the editor has to throw out a $1/4$-page feature and replace it by a $1/2$-page story.

When the editor says that he is going to use your story, but does not know when a slot will come up, he is telling the truth. Be patient.

The process varies greatly from one publishing house to another, but here is a typical example.

The subeditor marks up your manuscript, amending it to the house style, and sends it to the typesetters, who set and send the print outs (galleys) to the publisher's proofreader. The proofreader checks it for spelling mistakes which will be corrected by the typesetter. Increasingly, editors ask freelance journalists to submit copy on disk. This saves typesetting time. But check that your word processing software and disk format is acceptable for the publisher.

The production editor receives the corrected galleys. He selects the illustrations and instructs a layout artist on how to make up the pages, or makes them up himself. The galleys are cut and pasted on to cardboard templates, together with photocopies of the pictures, until everything fits. The page make-up can also be made on-screen (**desktop publishing**), usually by subeditors.

Often a word, a line or a paragraph has to be inserted to make the text fit into the allocated space. It looks odd if a column begins with the last line of a paragraph, so the production editor will pad out the text with a few extra words to fill the line.

The pasted pages, plus the floppy disk with the text (or the disk with the desktop published pages), are sent to the repro house who scan in the pictures and produce films of the pages. Print outs of the films (page proofs) are sent to the subeditor for approval, and then to the printers.

The printers produce a printing plate from the page film, then the publication is printed and later bound.

Your manuscript never gets further than the typesetters.

## WHO IS THE EDITOR?

Readers, as well as writers, imagine that the editor, an all-important powerful person, gets involved in everything. This is rarely the case. Except with small press magazines, the editor-in-chief doesn't normally sort through the slush pile and send out rejection slips. He or she may not even decide about whom to commission to do what.

Much of the work which freelances think the editor does is done by other people on the editorial staff: the deputy editor, features editor, commissioning editor, desk editor, subeditor, production editor, editorial assistant and so on. Who is responsible for what differs from publication to publication. In this book the word 'editor' refers to the editorial team in general, not to the person of the editor-in-chief.

Letters addressed to 'The Editor' are usually opened by a secretary and distributed to the other editorial staff, in an attempt to keep as much away from the editor as possible.

The masthead or colophon, too, can be misleading. It may not list the full editorial staff, and the name of the person responsible for freelance manuscripts may be not included. Or the list may be padded out with fantasy names to impress readers, advertisers and competitors. In some one-person operations the editor puts down his name as well as three different pseudonyms and four job titles.

Sometimes, the editor-in-chief's name is added for prestige reasons only, and the person in question has little involvement with the publication. This may be the case when the magazine publishers like the prestige of using a reputable expert's name, and the expert of having the title 'editor'.

So to whom do you address your letters? 'Dear Editor' is acceptable initially if you don't know the name of the person. All further correspondence and queries should be addressed to whoever signed the response.

## UNDERSTANDING EDITORS

It is often assumed that the editor is the most powerful person in the publishing house, that he decides what goes into the newspaper or magazine, thus influencing public opinion. This is not necessarily true.

Newspapers and magazines are financed mainly by advertising which provides about 80 per cent of the revenue, and according to the publisher's calculation, finance the editorial department including freelance fees. Subscriptions and over the counter sales pay for only 20 per cent – usually just enough to cover the distribution cost and postage. The advertising manager is often equal in rank to the editor.

Many advertisers are aware of their power and demand a nice editorial write up for their products, or threaten to cancel the annual advertising order if a friendly word about their competitors has been published.

Editors attempt to keep the editorial pages independent, despite the pressure from the advertising department. However, few publications can afford to ignore the advertisers' interests.

When I was deputy editor of a fashion magazine, we had the policy of 'two ed for one ad'. This meant that for every paid advertising page we had to publish two editorial pages promoting the advertiser. We fulfilled this condition by publishing photos of clothes from the advertiser's range, or perhaps an interview with their designer. In one case, the advertiser demanded that we published her sister-in-law's poems instead!

Sometimes we received a freelance manuscript along the lines How to Make Your Own Evening Gown. Our readers would have loved it – we had many readers' letters asking for information on the subject. But the main advertisers were producers of evening wear, and the DIY subject was taboo. Of course, we could not say so in the rejection slips.

### What editors may not tell you

Many publishers try to turn the editorial department into a moneymaking organisation, not only by selling editorial space as 'advertising feature'. Some accept articles only if someone pays a contribution towards the production (usually called 'separation charges').

For example, your travel article about an exotic country may be perfect for a magazine and its readers, but if the relevant tourist board refuses to pay separation charges for colour photos, the editor may reject it in favour of a less exciting article about a country which offers to pay.

Travel, home furnishing, fashion and cosmetics are the areas where separation charges have become a habit for many publications.

Few editors are happy with this situation. Freelances should know that these commercial interests can be the reason behind a rejection.

## HOW TO PLEASE AN EDITOR

Many freelances (particularly those whose ms have just been rejected) complain that editors are unfeeling, unfriendly, anonymous. But imagine yourself on the other side of the desk.

### How editors see freelances

Some freelance writers are pleasant to work with. They are reliable people, full of initiative and ideas, who support editors with their knowledge and competence and save them much time.

Others appear to be impatient, unfriendly people, who demand time, work, patience and money and don't even bother to say thank you. They cheat with their invoices, get the facts in their features wrong and the editor into trouble – in short, they are a nuisance.

It may seem incredible, but there are more freelances of the second kind. Most editors come to the point where they refuse to even look at anything freelance-written. Friendly communications from freelances are rare.

Few writers thank the editor who has made the effort of explaining why he had to reject it. Hardly anyone bothers to say they are proud to write for the magazine, or how stunning the layout of their latest article looks in print.

Instead, editors get many letters accusing them of not reading manuscripts properly. An equal number complain about a changed phrase, a cut paragraph, or a boring layout. Add to that the freelances who blame the editor if the accepted feature does not appear in the next issue or if a cheque is delayed, and those who keep hinting that they find the magazine 'rather amateurish'. You get the picture.

Editors are not immune to flattery. Praise their publication, or their comment column. Say that you like the headline and the illustration which they have chosen to go with your story. Mention a feature they have published recently, which you have read with enthusiasm. Tell them that you are happy to have your feature accepted, and proud to write for their 'prestigious magazine' (the latter is particularly welcomed by editors of lesser-known publications).

Many freelances hesitate to write a friendly word to the editor, for fear that their efforts could be regarded as sycophantic. However, among so many letters of criticism a friendly word is always welcome.

When I was acting editor of a trade magazine, I put much time and work into editorial guidelines and sent them all to prospective contributors. One of them reacted immediately. 'Your guidelines are the best I have ever seen,' he wrote. 'Comprehensive and extremely helpful. I look forward to writing for you.' When his feature suggestions arrived, I recognised his name immediately.

### Let the editor know – at once
Be reliable, and be honest. If the editor has expressed interest in your feature suggestion, and you have changed your mind and don't want to write it, let him know. If research takes up more time than expected and you feel that you can't make the **deadline**, contact the editorial department as soon as possible.

Write, rather than phone. Nothing annoys an editor more than phone calls when he is desperately trying to get pages ready for print. If you have to phone, don't ask for the editor personally. His deputy, the secretary, or the features editor can probably help you equally well. The best informed person in the department is usually the editorial assistant.

### Secret files
Editors often approach each other for information about a journalist: 'This journalist wants to write a regular column for us. Is he reliable?' or 'I am looking for a contributor to cover the South East. Can you recommend someone?'

Each editor has a contributors' file. This can be a card system, or a computer data base. In addition to factual information, such as name, address, telephone, specialist subjects and rates, editors add comments.

Here is a selection of comments from the freelance file I've carried with me to whichever publication I was editing.

'Reliable, but always tries to get more pay.' 'Well researched features, but never keeps deadlines.' 'Pleasant person, keen to get a byline.' 'Writes too much, charges too much.' 'Good style, shows initiative.' 'Does not follow briefing, ms full of errors and handwritten corrections.' 'Initiative, brilliant ideas, well researched; style needs subbing.' 'Constantly threatens to stop submitting if we don't pay more, but always comes back.' 'Makes even legal subjects sound interesting.' 'Competent, reliable and highly professional.'

What notes have *your* editors written about *you*?

## QUESTIONS AND ANSWERS

Q: Should I include the editors for whom I have written recently in my Christmas card list?

A: No. Sending a card would do no harm, but it is a waste of money. Every December the average editorial office is literally flooded with

Christmas cards, most of them from public relations people. Chances that your card stands out and catches the editor's attention are small.

Q: How long should I wait for an editor's decision about a feature?
A: There are no hard and fast rules. The editorial staff on some publications work faster than on others. It also depends on the time of the year – in some months they are busier than in others. Give it a couple of months if it was an on spec submission or suggestion; three weeks if the editor has asked to see it; less if the article is a topical one.

Q: Can I ask the editor to explain the reason for rejecting my feature?
A: Yes, if the editor has asked to see the feature. He will probably give an explanation if you ask politely and don't challenge his decision. No, if it was an on spec submission. It is not an editor's job to teach you how to write better features.

## KNOWING THE LAW

### Copyright
There is no copyright on ideas or facts. If you read a feature about an interesting subject, and think you can write it better, then there is nothing to stop you from writing a feature based on this idea for another magazine.

Think twice, however, before you copy facts from other journalists' articles. You might be copying their mistakes. Always try to trace the original source.

The way someone puts words together to create a text is protected by copyright. If you like the introductory sentence of somebody's feature, you cannot just use it for your own article.

However, you are allowed to quote short extracts from other people's work, as long as you make it clear that it is a quote, and give the source. The law is not precise about how long these quotes can be. In practice, most journalists restrict their quotes to three sentences.

The Society of Authors has produced a guide on copyright – see page 140.

### Libel
Think twice before you embark on a campaign to ruin somebody's reputation. If this person brings a libel writ against you, you may be ruined

financially. Libel laws are strict, and courts are likely to interpret them in the libelled person's favour. There is no affordable indemnity insurance which would protect freelance journalists.

However, you need not panic. If someone feels they have been libelled they can choose whether they take the bylined writer, or the editor, or the publisher to court. They usually choose the one from whom they can get most money. This is seldom the freelance scribe.

The laws are complex. Ask yourself: is what I'm writing likely to damage someone's personal or professional reputation? If yes, be careful. The exception is, of course, the article which is clearly marked as a review.

If you think that a piece you are writing is potentially libellous, point it out to your editor, who can advise how to handle the situation, for example by phrasing a sentence carefully.

Invest in the Society of Authors' guide to libel, or read the relevant section in the *Writers' and Artists' Yearbook*.

## WHAT EDITORS HATE ABOUT FREELANCE WRITERS

I asked several editors what their pet hate is about existing and would-be freelance contributors.

- Charles Donavan, features assistant, *Woman & Home*: 'Ignoring the brief, and not bothering to read the magazine.'

- Brian Lund, editor, *Picture Postcard Monthly*: 'Sending articles without checking if we have already published a similar article on the same subject in recent issues.'

- Pam Guilder, media relations manager, *Countryside*: 'Poor writing technique.'

- Stephen Garnett, deputy editor, *Evergreen*: 'Long CVs included with their work, lists of previously published work, lengthy involved letters, and obviously unsuitable material.'

- Frank Westworth, editor, *Classic Bike Guide*: 'Freelances who know more about my titles and their market positioning than I do. Freelances who promise features and then sell them to competing titles. Freelances who try to publish the same story more than once in competing titles. Freelances who lecture me about how I should do my job. Freelances who acquire my home phone number and call me in the middle of the night "for a chat".'

- Rob Keenan, features editor, *Amateur Gardening*: 'Not knowing who they are writing for.'

- Mick Whitworth, deputy editor, *The Grocer*: 'What annoys me most about freelances is failing to deliver, or not delivering to the brief. With a staff writer you know straight away if things aren't running smoothly. With a freelance it's much harder. Sometimes, as a deadline approaches, I get this strange sense of doom because I suspect the freelance is bluffing but I can't actually prove it. The best freelances give you genuine reassurance – you know the copy will arrive on time and the content will be 99 per cent on target.

  'Failing to write to the brief is unforgivable. If I've given vague instructions I can't complain if the result is dodgy. But if I've explained exactly what I want, who should be quoted and what angle to take, I don't expect to receive a watered-down version. I don't pay for stories that don't meet their brief.'

- Amanda Griffin, editor, *Stationery Trade News*: 'Missing deadlines, exceeding word-count limits, not following copy guidelines.'

- John T. Wilson, editor, *Great Ideas*: 'When their query letters are vague and they don't enclose an sae.'

## WHAT MAKES A GOOD FREELANCE JOURNALIST?

I asked editors to describe the type of freelance journalist with whom they like to work.

- Charles Donavan, features assistant, *Woman & Home*: 'Ideas.'

- Brian Lund, editor, *Picture Postcard Monthly*: 'Well-researched articles.'

- Pam Guilder, media relations manager, *Countryside*: 'Someone who grasps the scope of the job to be done, writes well, and delivers on time.'

- Stephen Garnett, deputy editor, *Evergreen*: 'The ability to write well and unpretentiously in a style, and on a subject, appropriate to the magazine/newspaper they are targeting.'

- Frank Westworth, editor, *Classic Bike Guide*: 'A good freelance will be familiar with the titles he/she hopes to contribute to. If a writer is familiar with a title, they will be able to spot where an editor is having to place freelance work because of staff limitations. They will be able to offer an editor features which will fit into the framework, which will improve it by adding to the readability of an issue, rather than standing proud of it. They should be able to write clear, clean English and submit both hard copy and disk or e-mail files. They will check their own facts and be accurate. They will understand that their work is more likely to be used if it comes as a complete package – that is words and pics. They should always understand that magazines are not democracies and that the editor is always right. Even if he/she plainly isn't....'

- Rob Keenan, features editor, *Amateur Gardening*: 'Someone who can work to tight deadlines and can write to a brief.'

- Amanda Griffin, editor, *Stationery Trade News*: 'Someone who can write to a brief by an agreed deadline and bother to ask the editor if they are going to, in any way, change a brief.'

# 10

## Illustrating Your Articles

### BUYING A CAMERA

Choose a camera which is lightweight, and quick and easy to handle. Autofocus cameras are ideal for freelance journalists. Choose one which has a zoom, enabling you to take pictures from a 'non-threatening' distance, which means that people behave more naturally when you photograph them. It is also easier to get around unwanted lamp posts and cars in the foreground.

Go for the best lens you can afford. Make sure the camera has a lens cap, if possible built in. Scratched lenses and lost caps are frequent problems.

Some camera shops sell good second-hand cameras with a six-month guarantee.

For most publications, including glossy magazines, pictures taken with small autofocus cameras are acceptable and reproduce well, provided they are sharp in focus.

A higher level of technical perfection is essential to get photos accepted for full-page size publication or for cover pages.

### THE SUBJECT COUNTS

Try to take several photos of every subject you write about. Editors like photos which show people in general, children, good-looking young women and men, animals and action, and depict atmosphere.

### A CRASH COURSE IN PRESS PHOTOGRAPHY

If you write about a business woman or a craftsman, show her or him at work – at the desk or the telefax, with the hammer or chisel. The article is illustrated much better with an 'action' picture rather than a shot where the person sits or stands stiffly, not knowing what to do with their hands.

When taking photos of a theatre play or dress rehearsal, show a colourful, dynamic scene with two or three people, rather than a stiff group shot.

Avoid pictures of mayors. They have several appointments per day and the readers of the local newspapers get bored with the same face on every page. Equally boring is the picture of two people standing parallel to each other while shaking hands – this is an unnatural pose. Avoid cheque presentations to charities; take a photo of the activity which raised the money instead.

When taking a shot of a general scene – say, a fun fair, a folk dance festival or a crowded beach on a hot summer's day – make sure you get people's faces rather than their backs. Focus on a small child. Take a picture which makes readers think 'how cute'. Alternatively, you can focus on a pretty young girl or a handsome bloke. They should come across as friendly and cheerful, with subtle sex appeal.

Travel editors are not interested in photos of landscapes and famous buildings, which are available free from tourist boards. Shots of native crafts people at work are bestsellers, followed by pictures of handsome men and women, cute children, and animals in their natural habitat.

Bright red is every picture editor's favourite colour. So watch out for red dresses in the crowd, red fruit at the market stalls, red shorts at the sports festival, red balloons in the sky.

## COLOUR OR BLACK-AND-WHITE?

Some publications use only colour (referred to as '4c'), some only black-and-white (b/w) photography. Is it possible for the editor to have colour pictures reproduced in black-and-white? It is. However, the result is not always satisfactory, and never as good as if the photo had been taken in black-and-white. Reasonable results can be achieved if the photo has strong light-dark contrasts and clear lines.

The printing procedure often requires that some pages are printed in 4c, others in b/w, which have to be in a specific order. Publishing a single 4c photo on a b/w page can mean, for example, that eight full pages have to be printed in 4c. This can cost a fortune, so don't be disappointed if your photo appears in b/w print although other parts of the magazine have been published in colour. Editors often have to decide at short notice which features to publish on 4c or b/w pages.

### When to choose transparencies
The reproduction quality from a slide or transparency ('tranny') is always better than from a print, particularly if the picture is to appear in

a large format. However, trannies are expensive, and if you don't want to send your originals you may have to spend a considerable amount to have them duplicated. Colour prints are acceptable for most publications, unless they are intended for a full page or the cover. Travel magazines often insist on trannies.

Unfortunately, it is not possible to have transparencies made from print film. If you have used print film only while you were in Sri Lanka, and the editor insists on trannies, there is nothing you can do. You could have your print photos photographed onto slide film, but the resulting quality won't satisfy an editor.

Some photographers send colour prints, noting on the reverse 'Tranny available on request'. This is a sensible and perfectly acceptable solution, except for urgent commissioned work.

## Does size matter?

Size is unimportant. Large prints give better reproduction quality, but are damaged more easily than small prints. Postcard size is usually a convenient solution.

The situation is more difficult with trannies: 50 per cent of all editors prefer the small, mounted format (which they can use in a projector), the other 50 per cent say that the larger size is more convenient on a light-box.

## TO CROP OR NOT TO CROP?

Many books and features on photography have one weakness in common: they are written by freelance photographers, not editors, and fail to present editorial requirements from the editor's point of view.

If you are serious about submitting your photos for publication, forget anything you have ever read about cropping, for example. Tight cropping, that is cutting away as much background as possible to create an unusual composition or to focus on the main motif, may earn you a prize in photographic competitions. But it will also, almost certainly, earn you a rejection slip from the editor.

Editors prefer as much background as possible, the more boring, the better. 'Unnecessary' background allows, for example, for cropping a 'landscape' (horizontal) format into a 'portrait' (vertical), a square or any other shape required by the layout, without cutting away any essential material. Editors frequently have to reject photos because they would need three more millimetres on either side – possibly the three millimetres the freelance has previously cropped to create a special effect.

A professional production editor has much more experience at cropping than you have, and will bring out your photos to their best advantage. Of course you can, alternatively, submit one portrait and one landscape version of each photo, but photos with a lot of background still stand a better chance of publication.

If you ignore the advice given in books on photography, and *don't* cut away that large chuck of boring, pale grey sky, the editor has the opportunity to print the headline, the introductory paragraph, or a caption into it, a layout style which is particularly popular with magazines. Of course, your main motif must be clear in focus and cover most of the picture. There's no use in sending a photo where the main subject accounts for only a tenth of the picture.

## CAPTIONING

If you can think of a witty caption, fine, but more importantly it must be informative. The editor will use the information supplied to write a caption which fits into the available space.

It is your job, not the editor's, to find out the names, titles and positions of all the people in the photo. Ask them as soon as you've taken the picture; it will be difficult to get the relevant information afterwards. Keep pen and notebook at hand. The caption must also contain the venue, the event, and the date when the picture was taken.

## SUBMITTING PHOTOS

Take care to label your photos correctly with photographer's name and address, subject pictured, title or caption suggestion, date when taken, full names and titles of all people in the photo, if and for how long the photo may be held in stock. Self-adhesive labels are better than ballpoint pens, which can damage the picture, and felt-tip pens or rubber stamps which tend to smear. Typed labels are preferred to handwritten notes. When submitting trannies, give the basic information on the mount or bag and number them (e.g. 'Smith – council meeting – 4') and attach a list with detailed information.

Take care with the packaging, use strong envelopes. You can buy cardboard-lined or padded envelopes, but it is cheaper to use ordinary ones and cut your cornflakes boxes into A5 size. A self-addressed, stamped envelope should be enclosed. As this can be difficult and expensive, you may use stamped, self-addressed 're-use envelope' labels instead. The editor can re-use the padded envelope in which you have sent the pics.

Ninety-nine per cent of all glass-mounted trannies arrive with broken glass, however well padded the envelope is. Cardboard or plastic mounts are safer and cheaper. And if you submit a series of trannies, the editors appreciate them in clear plastic presentation bags available in photo shops.

## HOW TO GET YOUR PICTURES BACK

Many photos and trannies get lost in the production process, either in the editorial office, at the lithographer's or the printer's. Always keep your negatives. You can have duplicates made from transparencies; this costs about £1.20 each. The dupes are usually very good, although the colours may not be quite as strong.

If you require your photos back after publication, write 'please return to. . .' on each of them. However, it can take weeks until the editors receive them from the repro house, and even longer until they find the time to return them to you.

## WHAT THE EDITORS SAY

Most editors want photos; most pay more for a feature with photos than for one without, but editors tend to be vague about how much they are willing to pay for pictures. If you get commissioned to produce a feature with illustrations, negotiate payment for pictures in advance. It can vary from 50 pence to £100 for each illustration. Here are some editors' statements:

- Charles Donavan, features assistant, *Woman & Home*: 'In principle, we like photos, but don't send them on spec. When we use your pictures with your article, we will pay extra for them.'

- John T. Wilson, editor, *Great Ideas*: 'I welcome black and white photos (or colour photos which can be reproduced in b/w) and line drawings. Payment is £5 per illustration.'

- Rob Keenan, features editor, *Amateur Gardening*: 'Yes, we want photos – preferably colour, medium format/slides.'

- Frank Westworth, editor, *Classic Bike Guide*: 'Yes, I want photos, in almost any format. I'll pay extra for them if they are professionally shot, or I may pay the photographer as well.'

- Stephen Garnett, deputy editor, *Evergreen*. 'Yes, I welcome photos, whether b/w, colour, slides or prints. We do pay extra. How much depends on the size we use the picture.'

# 11

## Managing Money Matters

### NEGOTIATING YOUR FEE

Freelance journalism is a buyer's market. Supply exceeds demand by far, and the buyers, the editors, dictate prices. As a freelance you have the choice to sell either at market price, or not at all. Rates vary greatly, with small press and women's magazines at the bottom and business and technical publications at the top end of the scale.

If bylines are more important to you than profit, or if a publication has standard rates, simply add to your query letter the phrase 'at your usual rates'.

Editors who say that payment is made 'by arrangement' expect an indication of your price range. The sentence 'My usual rates are between £60 and £120' shows that you are a professional.

The editor understands that for £60 you will supply a good feature, and for £120 probably an even better one. She also knows that if she can offer only £50, a compromise is possible, but if her maximum is £10 it is not worth wasting her time and yours

### Avoiding disappointment

Freelances and editors have one thing in common: a strong dislike for discussing the financial side. Freelances are afraid to appear greedy, while editors are embarrassed that they cannot afford to pay NUJ (National Union of Journalists) rates. But if payment is not discussed in advance, disappointment is inevitable.

Once I was present at the discussion between an editor and a prospective contributor. Every aspect of editorial requirements was discussed in detail, and only after two hours did it become clear that the freelance expected a minimum rate of £200, and the editor, with the best will in the world, could not afford more than £20.

Editors are grateful if you open the financial discussion frankly and at an early stage, to save time and embarrassment for both of you.

Most editors are aware of how much time and effort goes into freelance journalism and would like to pay good rates. However, their position is that of business managers, employed to buy the best possible material at the lowest possible price. The budgets are often very tight. If they buy your feature, they have to reject another one. If they agree to pay you a higher rate, they have to cut back on somebody else's.

Often, they are deeply ashamed that they cannot pay a freelance as much as his work is worth. Many freelances add to the embarrassment by assuming an arrogant smile and a contemptuous voice when talking about money matters, and this does not help.

If you are unsure how much to ask, begin the negotiation by stating your normal rates, perhaps with a wide 'between . . . and . . .' rate.

Maybe the editor will take the first step and quote a figure. If you think you could get more it is fair to say 'I had hoped for £120'. Freelances usually succeed if they ask for 20 per cent more than offered (if they have approached the editor with a feature), or even 50 per cent more (if the editor has approached them).

## GETTING AN INCREASE

As a regular contributor whose services have been valued over a considerable period, you'll probably be looking for a rise. This is a reasonable request, but the subject must be approached diplomatically.

If you tell the editor that you need the money because you have to feed a family and pay a high mortgage, she may feel for you, but is unlikely to give you an increase. Blackmail does not pay either.

When I was working for *European Frozen Food Buyer* and *European Drinks Buyer*, we paid £80/1000 words. Not a fortune, but not bad either. Some contributors wrote unpleasant letters threatening that unless we tripled the rates immediately they would stop submitting. They were quickly replaced. All of them, without exception, came back after a while, saying that they had not meant it so seriously and of course they would be happy to write at the usual rate . . . too late.

The one and only reason which will convince the editor to give you a rise is that you can give her a better product to justify the higher price. Explain what you could do even better than before if paid more, and how the publication would benefit from it: for example more detailed research, foreign contacts, manuscript submissions on disk, etc.

## GETTING PAID

Some publications pay on acceptance, but most on publication. Checking every issue, week after week, to see if your article is printed can be nerve-wracking! Always ask the editor to send you a free copy of the issue which contains your work.

While some publishers send a cheque automatically as soon as the article is printed, others require an invoice. It is a good idea to send out invoices anyway, because they create a professional impression. If you have registered your journalism business for VAT, you must send invoices in any case.

Invoices can be done on your computer or typewriter. You can also buy a duplicate invoice book, fill in the invoice forms by hand, send the original to the editor and keep the duplicate in the book. This is the quickest and most practical way.

Address your invoices to the person who has accepted the feature. It should contain the word 'invoice', your name and address, the invoice date and invoice number, the title of the feature, the dates of acceptance and publication, the length, the agreed rate, the overall price, and if applicable, VAT. You may add 'payable by' (insert a date four weeks after publication) to speed up payment.

## MAKING PUBLISHERS PAY SOONER

Don't cover several features with one invoice. Accountants are in the habit of paying small invoices quickly, and putting large invoices aside until some money comes in. If the company has a cash flow problem, they may spread payment of your ten invoices at £100 each over three months, but if you send one invoice for £1000 you may have to wait a year!

A number of accountants unfortunately tend to think of writers as artists who should not demand payment, and therefore regard writers' invoices as 'unimportant'. Send a business-like reminder, addressed to the accounts department, where your invoice and the chequebook usually are. It is not the editor's job, at least not in major publishing houses, to chase up overdue payments for you. The reminder should be polite, matter-of-fact, and repeat all the information contained in the invoice.

Four weeks' delay justifies a first reminder, eight weeks a second. After that, it is time for a phone call. Most freelances make the mistake of being very rude, and consequently unsuccessful. Learn from professional credit control people, who enquire in a pleasant tone: 'Good afternoon, I wonder if you can help me. My name is Cathy Clever, and my invoice dated 10 October is still outstanding. I wonder if there is a problem?'

Note that this is an enquiry, not an accusation. The accountant who remembers your friendly voice will find it more difficult to ignore your invoice. The phone call gives the company a chance to sort out a compromise. For example, if cash flow is their problem you may agree on payment by instalments.

# Invoice

| | |
|---|---|
| **Invoice number:** | 0015 |
| **Date:** | 28 November 199x |
| **Payable by:** | 31 December 199x |

**From:**
**Nigel Nickeling**
**1, Abcde Lane**
**Fghijkl Town YY1 1ZZ**
**Tel (0000) 00000**

**To:**
**You and Your House**
**Att. Doreen Dorian, Editor**

| Publication date | Item | Words/ Quantity | Rate | Amount |
|---|---|---|---|---|
| 15 November 199x | Feature 'How to make your home burglarproof' | 800 | 62.50/1000 | £ 50.00 |
| | Photo 'Installing window locks' | 1 | 20 | £ 20.00 |
| 22 November 199x | Feature 'How to save money on heating bills' | 1000 | 62.50/1000 | £ 62.50 |
| | Photos for illustration | 3 | 20 | £ 60.00 |
| | | | | £192.60 |

Fig. 19. Invoice.

# Reminder

**Date:** 15 January 199x

**Invoice number:**   0015
**Date of invoice**    28 November 199x
**Payable by:**        31 December 199x

**From:**
**Nigel Nickeling**
**1, Abcde Lane**
**Fghijkl Town YY1 1ZZ**
**Tel (0000) 00000**

**To:**
You and Your House
Att. Doreen Dorian, Editor

May I remind you that payment for the following items is now overdue:

| Publication date | Item | Words/ Quantity | Rate | Amount |
|---|---|---|---|---|
| 15 November 199x | Feature 'How to make your home burglarproof' | 800 | 62.50/1000 | £ 50.00 |
| | Photo 'Installing window locks' | 1 | 20 | £ 20.00 |
| 22 November 199x | Feature 'How to save money on heating bills' | 1000 | 62.50/1000 | £ 62.50 |
| | Photos for illustration | 3 | 20 | £ 60.00 |
| | | | | £192.60 |

Fig. 20. Reminder.

## Using the small claims court

If the publishing house has scheduled future contributions from you, you could and should simply say: 'I won't submit part four of my feature series until I have the money you owe me.'

This is customary in all types of business, and it works. The editors will cringe, because you are upsetting their work schedule. It's not usually their fault that payment is late, but they are often able to convince the accountants that your invoice should be paid.

If this doesn't help, write a final polite letter, say that unless you are paid in full within two weeks you will take the matter to the small claims court. Professional journalists know that this method works – probably because accountants take legal matters seriously.

Still unsuccessful? Most likely the publishing house is in serious financial difficulties. Take your case to the small claims court before it is too late. Obtain three sets of the forms from your local court or from the Citizens' Advice Bureau, and fill them in clearly. Your clients will receive an official request to pay you. If they still don't pay, you get in touch with the small claims court again, and they will issue a summons for your client to appear in court.

You have to pay a fee for the service as soon as you hand in the forms. The amount depends on the amount you are owed. However, your client has to refund the money to you, so you won't lose out.

Using the small claims procedure means you have to invest some money and time, but it works. I have had to take many clients to court – including some well-established glossy national magazines – and they all paid up when they received the summons to court.

If you experience regular problems in getting your money from a publishing house, stop writing for them.


## PRACTICAL ASSIGNMENTS

1. Buy an invoice book, or design an invoice form which you can use, or practise writing invoices on your computer or typewriter.

2. Go to the small claims court or to the Citizens' Advice Bureau and obtain several small claims forms, so that you have them at hand when you need them.

3. Talk to other freelance journalists to find out how much they earn per 1000 words, how much each of their clients are paying, and which publishers appear to be late payers or in financial difficulties.

# 12

## Going Freelance

### ARE YOU READY TO TAKE THE PLUNGE?

Becoming a full-time freelance journalist means starting your own business. This needs careful thought and preparation. Don't give up your full-time job until you have mastered the craft and established good contacts with editors. Most journalists slipped gradually into self-employment, writing articles in their spare time, while earning a regular income from a staff job.

It pays to enrol on a course on how to start your own business, as well as a course on marketing skills, or personal selling skills. A good book to read is *How to Start a Business From Home* by Graham Jones. You can also get free booklets from banks.

Ask yourself the following questions:

- Am I a good journalist? Have I mastered the craft? Do I have a portfolio of published work?

- Do I have the contacts and the markets? Do editors recognise my name as an expert in my field? Are they willing to buy more of my work?

- Do I have enough ideas for articles?

- Has my average income from writing in the last six months been at least £50 per 1000 words?

- Has 50 per cent or more of the work I have written in the last 12 months been accepted for publication?

- Am I willing to take the risk? Can I cope with irregular income? Do I have any dependants? Do I have financial reserves to live on until the money for published articles comes in?

- Do I possess the necessary marketing skills, and the assertiveness to sell myself and my work?

- Do I have the self-discipline to work 40 hours a week (or whatever target I have set myself), shutting out distractions such as neighbours calling, the pile of ironing in the corner and the tempting novel on the bedside table?

- Can I keep going when times are tough, when there is a period of nothing but rejection slips?

## RAISING THE FINANCE

Setting yourself up as a journalist needs little money. But you must have enough to pay for day-to-day expenses such as the phone bill and postage stamps, and a reserve to live on until money comes in.

One of the hazards of being a freelance journalist is that you don't get paid when you submit your work, but when it has been published. Many months may pass between acceptance and publication.

You may be eligible for financial help if you are setting up in self-employment. Who is eligible, who gives the finance, and the precise conditions vary from year to year and from county to county.

Grants, scholarships, sponsorships and awards may be available from enterprise agencies, chambers of commerce, town and borough councils, writers' groups, journalism organisations, arts councils. Don't be shy, ask for information. But ask before you start your business, otherwise you may unintentionally break some of the rules of eligibility.

## PRESENTING A BUSINESS PLAN

A business plan shows you – and any potential sponsor – how likely your enterprise is to succeed. Answer the following questions in detail to develop a basic plan.

1. What experience, knowledge, training or experience do you have? For example, your work experience at a magazine's editorial office, and your experience in writing freelance in your spare time.

2. What are your personal strengths (for example, determination, selling skills) and weaknesses (for example, shyness)?

3. Describe your product (articles and features), your customers (publications) and the consumers (readers). What benefits do the publications and the readers get from your articles?

4. What is your survival income? How much do you need to cover your personal expenditure?

5. What do you want to achieve, and when? For example, to sell 20 features in two months.

6. How often will editors buy your features? How many will be regular customers, and how many will be one-offs?

7. Who are your competitors (other journalists who write about the same subject)? What are their strengths and weaknesses, and how much do they earn per 1000 words?

8. How long does it take you to write a 1000-word feature? How long to research it? How much do you want to, or have to, earn per 1000 words?

9. Describe how you do market research. For example, studying magazines and newspapers.

10. Describe your marketing strategy. For example, writing query letters.

11. How much money will you invest in equipment?

12. How much profit (income minus expenses) do you have to make to break even?

13. How much time will you spend on marketing, and how much on administration (for example, keeping books, filing)?

14. How many features can you sell per month, realistically? How much money can you earn per month?

15. How many days, weeks or months are likely to pass before you receive the money you have earned?

16. Make a profit or loss forecast. This is a table which shows how much money you spend and earn each month. The difference between the two is your profit or loss. During the first few months you may make a loss, because you are investing in equipment. But after a few months you must make a profit, otherwise your business is not viable.

17. Make a cash flow forecast. This shows the money coming into, and going out of, your bank account and purse.

For example, the editor accepts a feature and promises to pay £200. You have earned £200, and enter it in the profit and loss. Two months later, you receive the cheque. Now you enter £200 in the cash flow.

Preparing cash flow and profit and loss forecasts takes time. It is easiest with pre-printed forms which you can get free from most banks.

## PAYING TAX AND VAT

As soon as you open your business, you must notify the Inland Revenue. You are due to pay income tax at the end of the business year. How much you pay depends on your income, expenses and profits. You must keep detailed books.

You also must register with the Contributions Agency and pay National Insurance contributions. If you are a full-time freelance journalist you register for Class 2.

You don't have to pay VAT unless your turnover exceeds a certain amount which you as a freelance journalist are unlikely to achieve. However, you may choose to register voluntarily. This means extra paperwork, but it allows you to claim back VAT on items you bought for your business. For example, if you bought an expensive computer, and don't expect to earn a lot during the first year of business, you may get a considerable VAT refund.

However, it is sensible to take professional advice, because paying VAT is a complex process. Any discrepancy in your tax return, however innocent, could lead to a lengthy investigation. The cost, in terms of stress and loss of potential earnings whilst you resolve matters with the VAT office, could outweigh the perceived benefits.

Details change frequently, but you can get free booklets which explain the ins and outs of VAT, income tax and National Insurance contributions in plain English.

## JOINING A PROFESSIONAL ORGANISATION

When you become a member of a journalists' or writers' organisation you get advice, support (usually moral, but in some cases legal too), information, motivation and contacts.

Most organisations demand that you are a semi-professional, or professional, writer. Some, like the Society of Authors or International

PEN, accept only writers who have had at least one book published for full membership. Others are open only to women (for example, the Society of Women Writers and Journalists or the Women Writers Network), or to journalists who specialise in a subject (for example, the British Guild of Travel Writers).

Members are entitled to print 'member of. . .' in their letterheads, which shows that you are a professional.

Writers who are not yet professionals may not join, although they can attend many events and seminars for a small fee.

The Society of Women Writers and Journalists offers 'probationary membership' for aspiring writers who have had only a few pieces published. Probationary members have the same benefits as full members (except they may not use it on their letterheads), and after two years they are expected to achieve semi-professional level and become full members. (For details of organisations see Useful Addresses.)

## SELECTING THE TOOLS OF THE TRADE

### Equipping your office for little money

You don't need a lot to set yourself up as a freelance journalist. Here is a selection of useful items. Only you can decide what you need immediately, and which purchases you want to postpone until later.

*Stationery*
- A lot of white A4 paper. Buy it in bulk from your local printer.

- Envelopes in varying sizes. You can get them much cheaper if you buy them in boxes of a thousand. Consider sharing a pack with other writers.

- Postage stamps. Except for topical news items, you can send out your queries and features second class and save money.

- A clippings book to keep your published articles in.

- Lots of suspension files, to file your published articles, sample features and research notes. Suspension files are cheapest if bought in packs of 50 or more.

- Box files, ringbinders and magazine files. Wait until your stationery supplier has them on special offer.

- Printed letterheads, with your name, address, and the membership of journalists' and writers' organisations. Shop around. Prices differ from printer to printer. By negotiating you often get a better deal. Five hundred letterheads, printed in one colour on good tinted paper, cost about £60 plus VAT. The more you order, the lower the price per sheet. The printer may charge you extra for the design.

- Compliment slips, similar in design and contents to the letterheads. Three hundred compliment slips cost around £25 plus VAT.

- Business cards. Instead of ordering them from your printer, use one of the instant print machines which you can find at many post offices and railway stations. At the printer's you would pay around £45 plus VAT for 200 cards. At the machine you get them for £3 per 50, including VAT.

*Office equipment*
- A typewriter. You can buy a good one second-hand at a car boot sale for under £15. Try it out, and make sure it is a brand for which ribbons are still available.

- A telephone. Ask British Telecom for an itemised bill if you are using your private phone for business purposes. If you decide to have a separate extension for your business, BT will charge you for the installation.

- A telephone answering machine, so that editors can leave a message at any time. You can buy one second-hand.

- A telefax machine. It's often cheaper to send a fax than to make a phone call, which helps keep down research costs, and faxes are great for urgent manuscripts. Telefax paper is cheapest if you buy at least five rolls at a time.

- Instead of a telefax, a telephone and a telephone answering machine, you can buy a machine which combines all three. Choose one which also allows you to take copies. These are not as good as proper photocopies, but the facility is useful when you're in a hurry. It should also have a facility to record your telephone conversations (for example, for telephone interviews). It is important that the machine recognises if an incoming call is a fax or a phone message, and switches automatically to either the fax or the answerphone when you're not there. Don't buy a combined machine second-hand: you have to switch manually from fax to answerphone and back, which is useless if an editor wants to send you a fax and you're not there.

● A word processor or computer, plus software and printer. (See below.)

*Furniture*
● A writing desk, perhaps with a return unit for your typewriter or computer. You can buy a good one from a dealer in used office furniture for around £50.

● A comfortable office chair, with adjustable height and back. You will spend a lot of time sitting at your desk. A second-hand office chair costs around £35.

● A mobile drawer unit for extra storage space, and on which you can place your printer or telefax (about £25 second-hand).

● A filing cabinet for suspension files (between £30 and £60 for a second-hand one with four drawers, depending on its condition).

## THE WRITER IN THE COMPUTER AGE

Word processing is increasingly important in journalism. This section introduces you to the basics you need to know about the subject. It helps you to decide if you want to buy a computer, and if so, which. But it cannot make the decision for you. Remember that computers and programs are updated frequently and prices change quickly. Regard this section as the starting point from which to start your own investigation.

### Do I need a computer?
You can be a successful writer without ever touching a computer. On the other hand, it is easier and quicker to make changes to a manuscript if you have it on your computer. For example, you can insert or delete whole sections, or move paragraphs around, without retyping the page.

With a computer you can produce more work during your working hours. This can help increase your income. On the other hand, computers are an expensive investment, and you have to write many features to recoup the money.

If the only reason why you are not earning a fortune is that you spend too much time retyping your manuscripts, then a computer is a worthwhile investment. But if you don't earn a fortune because all your manuscripts come back with rejection slips, then a computer won't help.

True, you can produce ten times as much work with a computer. If you normally write and sell two articles per week, you can write and sell 20 with a computer. But if you write two articles per week and they don't normally get published, then you will probably produce 20 articles per week which still won't get published.

## Do editors require word processed copy?

More and more editors welcome manuscript submissions on disks, which save typesetting costs. Some editors ask contributors if they have a modem to mail copy electronically. The use of modern technology in the communication between writers and editors is increasing. Submitting by e-mail is particularly useful if writing highly topical news articles, which would be out of date if you used the ordinary post. However, no magazine or newspaper editor will reject a good feature which arrives on his desk in traditional format.

## What do I need?

Even if you don't know anything about computers, you know – better than any computer dealer – what you are going to use it for, now or in future. Once you've made up your mind what you want to do, every good dealer can advise you on the best computer. Ask yourself:

- Am I the only person who will be using the computer? Are my spouse/children/employees going to use it?

- How many hours per day will I be using it?

- In addition to writing articles, what else will I do on the computer? Book-keeping? Desktop publishing? Games? Write a novel? Edit a newsletter?

- Do I want to exchange data (manuscripts) with editors? If so, what equipment do these editors use?

- Am I familiar with using computers? What experience do I have? How confident am I about learning new software?

- If I have never used a computer before, how confident am I?

● If I need tuition, where can I get it and how much is it going to cost?

● What is the maximum I can afford to pay?

Once you are clear in your mind, you can start shopping around. The items you need are a computer, a printer, a screen, a keyboard and word processing software. Often, you get a good deal if you buy a package which contains some or all of these items. However, the printer is seldom included in package deals and it is one of the most expensive items.

Make sure that the screen is a non-glare, low radiation one. You will be spending a lot of time at the computer. The keyboard should be a special hardwearing model – even the busiest secretary doesn't type as much non-stop as a writer does.

### Where do I buy a computer?

Just pop in to some computer stores, explain what you want and ask questions. Chain stores tend to offer lower prices, but less expertise and after-sales service. The same applies to computers bought by mail order.

When comparing prices, ask what period of warranty is included. If you have to pay extra for extended warranty it makes the purchase more expensive.

Choose a supplier whom you trust, and avoid those who talk to you in an arrogant or patronising tone. Ask other writers where they bought their computers, and how pleased they are with their purchases and the after-sales service.

### What computer do I need?

This depends on what you want to do with it. Many journalists are happy with PCWs (from Amstrad). Their main advantage is that they are more affordable than personal computers or Applemacs. The disadvantage is that their disk format is not compatible with other computers, so you cannot exchange disks with an editor.

Applemacs (from Mackintosh) are considered to work fast and to be especially strong on graphics and design. This is why many publishers, especially newspapers, use them in their editorial departments. It seems that the newspapers publishers' preferred software packages for Applemacs are WordPerfect (for word processing) and Quark XPress (for desktop publishing). Applemacs are relatively expensive. Their disks can be used only on other Applemacs, not on personal computers.

Personal computers (PCs) are probably the most versatile option.

Most of them are compatible, which means they can use the same software and disk formats. Prices depend on the brand name, the memory and many other factors. For journalism, you don't need much memory capacity, but if you are thinking of doing desktop publishing it is better to buy a computer with sufficient memory.

Choose a PC which has a hard disk drive (on which you do your work) as well as a 3.5" disk drive (so that you can take file and backup copies, and send disks to editors). You don't need an extra CD ROM drive for journalistic work.

## How do I choose my software?

The only software you need for journalism is one for word processing. You must buy a version which has been designed for your particular computer. A basic word processing software program which costs around £40 is sufficient for writing and editing articles. More sophisticated programs offer desktop publishing facilities and other extras. Some allow you to draw graphs to illustrate your business features with the latest data.

Word processing software packages are either DOS based or Windows based. DOS-based software tends to be quicker to use, but Windows-based software is easier to learn. Of the DOS word processing software, WordPerfect is the one most frequently used by editors. Among the Windows-based versions, AmiPro is the market leader, followed by Microsoft Word and WordPerfect for Windows.

Your software should have a spell-checker. The more vocabulary a spell-checker has, the faster it works, but the more mistakes it overlooks.

You can also buy additional grammar checker and writing style improving software. These can pick up the grammatical slips you make when you write quickly, and point out over-long sentences and other weaknesses.

## Can I buy a second-hand computer?

Yes. You can get them from computer auctions, through adverts in the local newspaper, even at car boot sales. Second-hand computers are cheap, but not guaranteed. Many computer dealers stock second-hand computers, but you have to ask because they prefer selling you a new one. Dealers can check second-hand computers expertly and offer a warranty.

## How can I get software cheaply?

Don't copy somebody else's software – it's illegal. You can buy second-hand software, but it is difficult to check that it is working well, and there is always the risk of viruses. When buying second-hand software, make sure you get a legal, registered copy, complete with handbooks.

The cheapest way of getting new, good software is to buy old versions from the producers. Every software program is updated once a year or so, and the old versions are sold at a lower price. For example, you may get version 03 for £90, whereas version 04, which has a few minor extras, costs £350.

If you want to buy several programs – say, one for word processing, one for spreadsheets, one for accountancy and one for desktop publishing – you can often get amazing deals on packages.

### Should I buy a desktop publishing program?

You don't need desktop publishing for journalism. However, many professional journalists do related work, for example edit corporate magazines and newsletters, using desktop publishing. Most of the sample letters in this book were produced using PageMaker desktop publishing and the clipart library of CorelDraw.

### How compatible are software programs?

Perhaps each of the publications for which you write uses a different system and different software. Is it possible to transfer information from one system to another?

Yes. Many of the bigger publishing houses have these facilities, or their typesetters or printers have them. However, it is not worth going through the process of transferring data this way for a single two-paragraph article.

Some editors ask for manuscripts in ASCII format. ASCII is the esperanto of the computer world. Imagine that your computer speaks one language, and your editor another, and they don't understand each other. But they both understand a third language, ASCII.

You write your articles as usual in your word processing software, but before you copy it onto a floppy disk for your editor you save it in ASCII format. Check with your software handbook if it is possible. Your editor's computer then translates the text from ASCII into the software used there.

### Is it true that working at computers can affect the health?

Yes. Like almost every other type of work, computing can cause health problems, especially if you sit at your computer day after day, for hours on end.

Make sure that the keyboard and the screen are in an ideal position to avoid repetitive strain injury in the wrists, or stiff neck and shoulders. Select a comfortable, back-supporting chair with adjustable height. Prefer low radiation monitors. You can also buy anti-glare screens to cover your monitor. If sunlight falls in at an angle which makes it difficult to read the screen during certain times of the day, draw the curtains.

Try to break up your computer work for five minutes every hour. Make that essential phone call or get a cup of coffee. It's easy to get carried away when you are in the middle of a feature, and forget to take a break.

If your eyes get tired, your wrists or shoulders ache and you get a headache, take a break immediately. Either do writing-related work for which you don't need the computer (market study, filing) or go for a short walk.

## USING THE INTERNET

There are two problems about doing research on the Internet. One is, that you run up enormous bills to get the same information as you could get for free at your local reference library. The other is that the information is, on the whole, dubious.

I have studied several sections of the Internet, related to subjects about which I know more than most people – such as belly dancing. I found that over 50 per cent of all the information was either false or hopelessly outdated. Some was ridiculous, some even libellous. You don't want to copy other people's errors and undermine your credibility, or be sued for libel. This is because anyone can feed any information into the Internet, with very few control and editing mechanisms in place.

I'm not saying don't use the Internet. Perhaps you are connected to it anyway, perhaps you simply enjoy surfing the net, or maybe you are mobility impaired and can't go to the library or meet people to do your research.

But be careful about the information you find. Always check the source. If you know who has supplied the information, you may be able to judge if it is likely to be valid.

Use the Internet as a starting point for your research, to get a rough idea of what information sources there are, then approach those sources directly for the latest update.

As for the money factor, I find it cheaper to pay a friend for the occasional search and printouts, than to be connected to the Internet myself.

# Glossary

**Article**. A piece of journalistic writing, usually short and topical.

**Boxed item**. A piece of factual information (contacts, phone numbers, figures) added to a feature, often printed in a frame.

**Bullets**. The dots at the beginning of paragraphs. Often used as a design element in magazines, for example in how-to articles. Journalists indicate bullets with asterisks in their manuscripts.

**Byline**. A published line identifying the writer, for example 'By Cathy Clever'.

**Caption**. The text which explains the contents of a picture.

**Commissioned**. Articles written 'to order' for an editor who gives detailed instructions and promises to buy the completed work at an agreed price.

**Copy**. Journalistic jargon for text.

**Deadline**. The date by which you must submit the finished article or feature.

**DTP; desktop publishing**. Computer programs used by most publishing houses to design and make up pages on screen, instead of the traditional method of pasting paper on cardboard. PageMaker and Quark Xpress are popular with publishers.

**Expenses**. The money you spend to research and write your article, for example train tickets to meet an interviewee. Some (but not all) editors pay expenses on top of the rate if the work is commissioned.

**Feature**. A piece of journalistic writing which deals with a subject in depth, not necessarily topical, but usually longer than an article. There is no strict division between articles and features. For some newspapers, every piece of more than 250 words is a 'feature'. Others draw the dividing line between 'article' and 'feature' at 2500 words.

**Freebie**. Samples of products or services given to journalists to try out free, to encourage reviews.

**House style**. A sheet for staff and freelance writers with information about which words, spellings and so on the publication prefers.

**Intro**. The first paragraph of a journalistic piece, often printed in bigger or bolder typeface than the rest. Must capture the reader.

**Ms; manuscript**. The typewritten text you submit to the editor.

**On spec**. On speculation. Sending a manuscript to an editor without guarantee that it will be bought.

**Proof**. Print out of the typeset work. Usually checked (proofread) by subeditors or proofreaders.

**Sae; stamped, addressed envelope**. Must be enclosed with every manuscript submission (except commissioned work, or features which the editor has asked to see). Large enough, and with sufficient postage, for the return of your work.

**Story**. Journalistic jargon for feature or article. Don't confuse with the fictional short story.

**Syndication**. Selling the same article or feature several times, to non-competing publications, for example to magazines in different countries.

# Further Reading

## BOOKS

*Writing for Publication*, Chriss McCallum (How To Books). This book
is packed with advice on all aspects of freelance writing, from query
letters to short story competitions, manuscript layout, agents and the
law of libel. It contains a surprising amount of comprehensive information for a compact book format, and is clearly structured. Warmly
recommended to beginners, as well as to experienced journalists who
want to explore other forms of writing.

*Writers' and Artists' Yearbook* (A&C Black). This contains addresses,
for example publications in the UK and abroad, complete with fre-
quency, editor's name address, telephone number, retail price, and
often the rates of pay and the type of work requested. The addresses
of syndication agents are valuable for professional journalists. The
second half contains information on law, tax, societies and prizes.
This book is updated every year.

*The Writer's Handbook*. Similar, but more focused on journalists' and
writers' requirements. Updated annually.

*1000 Markets for Freelance Writers*, Robert Palmer (Piatkus). This
book describes magazine markets only, and in more depth than *The
Writer's Handbook* and the *Writers' and Artists' Yearbook*. It gives
more information for the freelance journalist, such as rates of pay,
editors' specific requirements, typical reader. It covers magazines
only (not newspapers) and unfortunately it is not updated
frequently.

*Copyright & Law for Writers*, Helen Shay (How To Books). Written by
a solicitor cum freelance writer, this is the best book on the subject
available. Read it and stay clear of copyright and libel pitfalls.

*Starting to Write*, Marina & Deborah Oliver (How To Books). A good
book for absolute beginners, practical and motivating.

*Writing Reviews*, Carole Baldock (How To Books). If you enjoyed your
review writing exercise and want to specialise in this field, this book
gives you practical tips, inspiration, and an insight into what the work
of a reviewer really involves.

## BOOKLETS AND BROCHURES

*Directory of Writers' Circles*, from Jill Dick, Oldacre, Horderns Park Road, Chapel en le Frith, Derbyshire SK12 6SY, regularly updated (currently £5, but send sae for current price).

The Society of Authors offers a series of information booklets and quick guides for writers. Of particular interest are those on copyright, libel, the small claims court, buying a word processor, selling your writing, income tax, VAT. They cost betwen £1 and £3. Send sae for an up-to-date leaflet of what's available. Publications Department, The Society of Authors, 84 Drayton Gardens, London SW10 9SB.

## MAGAZINES

*Amateur Gardening*, Westover House, West Quay Road, Poole, Dorset BH15 1JG, Tel: (01202) 440840, Fax: (01202) 440860, e-mail amateurgardening@ipc.co.uk.

*Classic Bike Guide*, PO Box 101 Craven Arms, Shropshire SY9 5WA, Fax: (01588) 630193, e-mail classbikes@aol.com.

*Countryside*, The Countryside Commission, John Dower House, Crescent Place, Cheltenham GL9 1LA, Tel: (01242) 521381, Fax: (01242) 584270.

*Evergreen*, PO Box 52, Cheltenham GL50 1YQ, Tel: (01242) 57775, Fax: (01242) 222034.

*Great Ideas*, Business Innovations Research, Tregeraint House, Zennor, St Ives, Cornwall, TR26 3DB.

*Picture Postcard Monthly*, 15 Debdale Lane, Keyworth, Nottingham NG12 5HT, Tel: (0115) 937 4079.

*Stationery Trade News*, Peebles Publishing Group Ltd, 8 Thorney Leys Business Park, Witney, Oxon OX8 74E.

*The Grocer*, William Reed Publishing Ltd, Broadfield Park, Crawley, West Sussex RH11 9RT.

*The New Writer*, PO Box 60, Cranbrook, Kent TN17 2ZR.

*Writers News*, PO Box 4, Nairn IV12 4HU.

# Useful Addresses

Please enclose sae with your enquiry.

## COURSES

Morris College of Journalism, The Old School, Princes Road, Weybridge, Surrey KT13 9DA, Tel: (01932) 850008, Fax: (01932) 850805.

The Old Rectory Adult Education College (residential writing courses with Christine Hall), Fittleworth, Pulborough, West Sussex RH20 1HU, Tel/fax: (01798) 865306,
e-mail: oldrectory@mistral.co.uk,
web site: http://3.mistral.co.uk/oldrectory/index.html.

Urchfont Manor College, Urchfont, Devizes, Wiltshire SN10 4RG, Tel: (01380) 480495, Fax: (01380) 840005,
web site: http://www.aredu.org.uk/urchfontmanor.

## ORGANISATIONS

The British Guild of Travel Writers, c/o Mike Gerrard, 5 Parsonage Street, Wistow, Huntingdon, Cambridgeshire PE17 2QD.

The Society of Authors, 84 Drayton Gardens, London SW10 9SB, Tel: (0171) 373 6642, Fax: (0171) 373 5768,
e-mail authorsoc@writers.org.uk.

The Society of Freelance Editors & Proofreaders, Mermaid House, 1 Mermaid Court, London SE1 1HR, Tel: (0171) 403 5141, Fax: (0171) 407 1193, e-mail: admin@sfep.demon.co.uk,
WWW: http://www.sfep.demon.co.uk

The Society of Women Writers & Journalists, c/o Geraldine Beare, 39 Victoria Road, Knaphill, Woking, Surrey GU21 2AU.

Women Writers Network (WWN), Cathy Smith, Membership Secretary, 23 Prospect Road, London NW2 2JU.

# Index

## WRITING FOR PUBLICATION
**How to sell your work and succeed as a writer**

Chriss McCallum

Absorbing and highly informative, this is the fourth edition of Chriss McCallum's popular handbook. No author seriously interested in getting published can afford to be without this book. 'Handy for both professional and newcomer alike.' *Writers News*. 'Excellent.' *Competitors Journal*. Really definitive . . . Leaves every other similar book in its shade.' *Pause* (National Poetry Foundation). Chriss McCallum has many years' experience as a professional editor, working for several leading publishers.

*192pp illus. 1 85703 226 8. 4th edition.*

## STARTING TO WRITE
**How to create written work for publication and profit**

Marina & Deborah Oliver

This book shows would-be writers how to set realistic objectives, and how to devise a plan of action without wasting time and resources. Illustrated throughout with case studies, it will show you how to explore various options, discover what methods work best for you, and take advantage of tips from experienced writers. Start now, and learn how to get your work into print.

*124pp illus. 1 85703 401 5.*

## AWAKENING THE WRITER WITHIN
**How to discover and release your true writer's voice**

Cathy Birch

Your true writer's voice is unlikely to inhabit the realms of logic. Through guided visualisation, dream-work, astrology, tarot, word association and other 'sleight of mind' techniques, this book takes you on a journey into the subconscious to help find that voice – and use it. Cathy Birch is a Jungian psychotherapist, writer and lecturer. Her writing credits include series for Schools' television, comedy material for Bob Hope, Dave Allen, Marti Caine and the two Ronnies, and three language skills textbooks. Her poetry, articles and short stories have appeared in a variety of magazines and anthologies.

*144pp illus. 1 85703 281 0.*